Women in America

FROM COLONIAL TIMES TO THE 20TH CENTURY

Women in America

FROM COLONIAL TIMES TO THE 20TH CENTURY

Advisory Editors
LEON STEIN
ANNETTE K. BAXTER

A Note About This Volume

Having chosen a life of service in preference to a life in high society, Grace Hoadley Dodge (1856-1914) worked in the later years of her life to establish a unified Young Women's Christian Association. Earlier, she had organized the Industrial Education Association, which led ultimately, through the cooperation of Columbia University President Frederick Barnard, to the chartering of Teachers College. In the 1880s, Grace Dodge organized an informal group of women shop, factory and store workers that met once a week to discuss life's problems. She addressed the first book in this volume, an outgrowth of these meetings, "To my dear friends and fellow members of the 38th Street Working Girls' Society" and in a mixture of idealism and practical good sense advised and cautioned them about big city life. The second book, published five years later, is an anthology of the responses written by members of the 38th Street Working Girls Society. Reflecting the discussions, they are filled with hope and heartbreak and deal with such subjects as ideal womanhood, purity and modesty, education and books. The third part of this volume is the issue of the *Teachers College Record* devoted to Grace Hoadley Dodge.

Grace H. Dodge

HER LIFE AND WORK

ARNO PRESS

A New York Times Company

NEW YORK – 1974

Reprint Edition 1974 by Arno Press Inc.

WOMEN IN AMERICA
From Colonial Times to the 20th Century
ISBN for complete set: 0-405-06070-X
See last pages of this volume for titles.

Publisher's Note: This volume was
reprinted from the best available copies.

Manufactured in the United States of America

———◆———

Library of Congress Cataloging in Publication Data
Main entry under title:

Grace H. Dodge: her life and work.

    (Women in America: from colonial times to the
20th century)
    Reprint of A bundle of letters to busy girls on
practical matters, by G. H. Dodge, first published in
1887 by Funk & Wagnalls, New York; of Thoughts of busy
girls, edited by G. H. Dodge, first published in 1892
by Cassell Pub. Co., New York; and of Grace Hoadley
Dodge, from Teachers College record, v. 16, no. 2,
Mar. 1915.
    1. Young women. I. Dodge, Grace Hoadley, 1856-
1914. A bundle of letters to busy girls on practical
matters. 1974. II. Dodge, Grace Hoadley, 1856-1914,
comp. Thoughts of busy girls. 1974. III. Teachers
College record, v. 16, no. 2. IV. Series.
HQ1229.G77 1974   301.41'2'0924 [B]   74-3987
ISBN 0-405-06100-5

CONTENTS

A

BUNDLE OF LETTERS

TO

BUSY GIRLS

ON

PRACTICAL MATTERS.

*WRITTEN TO THOSE GIRLS, WHO HAVE NOT TIME OR
INCLINATION TO THINK AND STUDY ABOUT
THE MANY IMPORTANT THINGS WHICH
MAKE UP LIFE AND LIVING.*

BY

GRACE H. DODGE.

FUNK & WAGNALLS.

NEW YORK: LONDON:
18 & 20 ASTOR PLACE.   1887   44 FLEET STREET.

All Rights Reserved.

TO MY DEAR FRIENDS AND FELLOW MEMBERS OF
THE 38TH STREET WORKING GIRLS' SOCIETY,
I DEDICATE THESE LETTERS IN MEMORY
OF THE MANY HAPPY TUESDAY
EVENINGS WE HAVE SPENT
TOGETHER IN

"PRACTICAL TALK."

CONTENTS.

INTRODUCTION.

YEARS ago questions relating to woman's life in the home began to impress me with their importance. I found how little I knew and how little I had thought of the duties of daughter, sister, wife, mother, and the responsibilities that come to woman.

In talking with other girls, the same state of mind was discovered. We formed, therefore, classes for practical study which proved of great advantage to us.

After a while the idea developed of meeting with other girls certain evenings of the week—girls who, busy all day in factory, shop, or office, had not time for household life and thought.

A number responded to the first invitations, and for four years from twenty-five to a hundred girls, younger and older, met on Tuesday evenings for "Practical Talks."

These gatherings grew into the first Working Girls' Society, and this started similar organizations. In connection with these, the Tuesday evenings continued with added interest.

It was found that lectures were not appreciated and rarely understood ; but simple talks or discussions made deep impressions, and were sources of profit to many a young woman. A number have married, and now testify to the advantages of this sort of preparation for the duties of housekeeper, wife, and mother.

Some months ago it was suggested that the talks should be put in print, and I was requested to write some letters, giving, in simple form, thoughts which could be sent to those who cannot share the advantages of our gatherings.

These letters, therefore, go out bearing the mark of no literary skill—rather that of almost too familiar language ; but it is such as we use, and so will be understood by the girls who are addressed in them.

Necessarily there are certain repetitions, for the same ideas must come up under different heads ; and also it must be recognized that here are only summaries of talks which occupied the evenings of many months.

It is hoped that these will form the basis of similar gatherings, and that from the ideas thrown out others may be roused to think about them, and to meet to discuss matters which so closely affect us as women.

A BUNDLE OF LETTERS.

REASON WHY—HEALTH.

DEAR GIRLS :

For several winters we have had pleasant evenings together, discussing many personal and practical matters, and at the request of a few of you, I
am going to put some of our talks into letter form,
so that we can have them to refer to, and to consider more closely.

We are girls or young women, all of us busy,
with little spare time, and yet having room in our
lives for many thoughts and interests.

Some of these are perplexing and troublesome ;
others, full of bright anticipation and joy. We
all expect to grow older, and hope to have some
day homes of our own, where as wife and mother
we can be queen of some larger or smaller place and
centre.

We go to school to be educated, to fit ourselves for certain phases of our future, or to enable us to enjoy things that will come to us, as books and letters. But we found in our talks that we often neglected to think of preparing ourselves for the positions we each expect to fill, and never realized that it required any preparation to become the capable head of a family, or a strong, helpful woman.

Many of our friends marry and set up housekeeping, and all seems most prosperous. If, however, we know them well enough they will confide to us how hard the work is, how hard it is to make the money go far enough, how miserably sometimes they feel, how difficult it is to do as they wish they could do. If these friends had only prepared themselves for what has come to them to do, how much better it would be now!

In our Tuesday evening talks we have taken up practical matters, and by our discussing them, and talking over ways and means, we have been fitting ourselves for duties that will probably come to us. First as to ourselves: God, our Heavenly Father, has given to each of us, as His first gift, " *ourselves.*" This may seem funny, but it is true.

Our bodies are from Him, a beautiful house to hold us ; we are entrusted with the gift, and have to take care of it. How do we do this ? How are we making it ready for a happy, long life ? First, let us always remember that we have a furnace that has to be kept heated and in full working order, or we must suffer. Especially in the morning is it necessary to start the fire well, and to do this we must put in coal, not wood. The latter would burn for a while and then go out, but coal well lighted goes on burning for a long time, bringing warmth and cheer. By the furnace we have learned to recognize our stomachs, and know that food is meant by coal and wood.

Breakfasts are important ; we need to eat more than a bit of bread and cup of tea or coffee. These would act as kindling wood, burn, or satisfy us for a short time, and quickly would be used up. So often we girls say, "Oh, I oversleep, I wake up just in time to hurriedly dress, and I have not time to eat breakfast!" We must wake earlier and give ourselves time for breakfast. We need something hearty—oatmeal, hominy, a bit of meat, a potato, etc.—to fill the furnace and to give a start to all the wonderful machinery of our bodies. Then at noon a cream cake, a pie, a bun, candy, or some other little dainty seems to be the only thing we can eat or crave. A glass of milk, a hard-boiled egg, a meat sandwich, or something even heartier seems hard to eat, and we take the wood again instead of coal ; for how far do you think a cream cake and apple will go in preparing you for an afternoon of work ? The hearty things do not cost more money, but they do cost more thought and effort ; but the trouble will pay, and our digestions for all the future will be better for the trouble we take in preparing the lunch. I hope that we will try and remember a few simple rules as to the fuel needed to run the furnace which starts and keeps going the other machinery, which, in its turn, supports and runs us ourselves.

First. Eat a hearty breakfast, giving to it sufficient time. Second. Dinner or lunch must consist of something solid. Third. Eat as well as drink, and while tea and coffee in small quantities will not hurt us, many cups of either must make us nervous, and our furnaces will rebel if we fill them simply with liquids. Fourth. Let the stomach rest

part of the time, and not by constant nibbling of
fruit, cake, or candy keep it at work with nothing really to work upon. Fifth. Food must be
taken as slowly as possible, and taken in decent
order. Those of us who board or have furnished
rooms must specially guard ourselves, and remember that food is important and must be considered,
even if we do not care for it

Now to the outer body. Here we come to
water and its use. I know how difficult it is
sometimes to secure sufficient water, and how, in
consequence of this and the smallness of our
rooms, we find it hard to take baths. If we can,
however, we should take sponge baths, for the
little pores of the skin need opening constantly, so
that there will be no danger of their being closed,
thus preventing the passage of impure matter from
the body.

Every night we breathe out also much of this
matter, and quickly exhaust all the fresh air. We
must therefore let some air in to take the place of
that which is exhausted, and we must not sleep with
our heads covered with bedding. If we do this,
we breathe in the same air we have breathed out,

and receive no refreshment. Headache, languor, and general miserable feelings in the morning come from sleeping with no freshness of air, and if we persist in this our health is often seriously affected.

But how can we get air fresh enough ? First. Let the floor or house be well aired every morning by opening the windows. Second. Air again before going to bed. Third. Leave, if possible, the window open at the top all night. This can be done in the sitting-room or kitchen, if we have no window in our bedroom, and then have the doors opened through. If it seems too much of a draft, do as is often done in a sick-room : a piece of flannel or open cloth is taken and nailed on the sash, and the window opened a foot or more. The upper end of the flannel is then nailed to the window-frame. Air comes through, and no draft. When one wishes the window closed, the flannel will be in a heavy fold, which can hang out outside, and will not look badly from the room.

Another idea is to put a piece of wood on to the window, and shut it on that, so leaving air to come from a large crack between the two sashes.

The dress to cover the beautiful house which

contains us we will speak of in another letter.
Now we want to think of other hints which need
our thoughts.

Many of us suffer from constipation. We have
appointments or are due at work at seven, eight,
or nine, and find it hard to allow time for attend-
ing to ourselves. We let it go for a day, then
another, and so on. After a short time our system will not act as it should. A bad habit has
been formed. Constipation is the result. Let us
be careful of what pills or medicines we take. Use
natural means as far as possible, or, if it is necessary
to take anything, let it be something we know
all about, some licorice powder or other simple
remedy. But prevention is better than cure, so
let us try and care regularly for ourselves early in
the morning. Carelessness in this respect is at the
root of very many of our ailments. Then, while at
work we must not feel that we can accustom our
system to going without relieving itself in another
way. Agonies have been suffered by some of you
because you thought you could go without caring
for yourselves, being ashamed to leave work or to
go where you could find relief. In consequence

you allow hours to go by, and often lay the foundations of disease. We are girls, and want to be pure, modest women ; but we must also remember health, and how hard it is to regain this if once lost.

Here may we not pause for a moment and consider another matter. Every few weeks there come three to four days when we do not feel as well as usual. Oh, dear girls, at these times we want to guard ourselves from taking cold, avoid bathing in either fresh or salt water, and from the sun, or extreme cold ! The body is weakened, and liable to cold or other more serious trouble, if care is not taken. As for exercise, we busy women cannot often stop from work at such times, but we can do just as little as is absolutely necessary. It pays those days to spend ten or twenty cents for car fares, and in the evening to go early to bed, and not to go out. Dancing or violent exercise, heavy lifting, or any extra exertion must be avoided.

Hundreds of women have suffered all their lives from some foolish forgetfulness or carelessness about themselves when young.

If at these times we suffer greatly, especially at

night, we will find hot water very helpful and rest-ful. A bottle or tin lunch canister filled with very hot water placed on our back or stomach will relax the muscles and lighten the pain. A rubber-bag is also used in this way, or heated brick. If the bottle is selected, be very careful that the cork is pressed in tightly, for often the water escapes, and a wet bed is the consequence.

Sleep : we girls do not get enough of it ; but do let us secure all we can, and not try to sew, read, or do other things after ten o'clock. We need from seven to nine hours to give rest and refresh-ment to our beautiful home. It must be consid-ered, or the *we* that lives within will suffer. Some think every hour saved from sleep is so much pure gain. Rather it is pure loss, and a loss that will be felt, even though perhaps not for a long time.

The eyes or windows of the house need care. Try and not use them at twilight or with dim light, and remember to have the gas or candle placed so the light shines on book or work, and the shadow on the eyes.

Then the skin : besides being clean, it wants to be free from all impurities. Many washes, salves, and patent cosmetics for the complexion are ruinous, and will bring upon us all sorts of trouble.

We have sometimes asked among ourselves, How can we make our hair beautiful? A Quaker friend answered me when I asked her the question by saying, "Use plenty of elbow grease.". When I asked her to explain, she said, " Oh, I mean give the hair a hundred strokes from the brush each night, and use the elbow hard in giving them !" None of us have time for a hundred strokes, but we can give some, and use only on the hair-brush and comb, with a thorough washing of the head and hair once in every two or three months.

Teeth need care, too, and brushing with a simple powder and plenty of fresh water is necessary to keep them in good order.

Let us here think of another thing, and that is, while dentists and doctors are dreaded persons both on account of their advice and their expense, yet they are necessities. By consulting them soon they will not become so dreaded. Leaving the dentist or doctor until we cannot bear the pain or misery longer is a bad habit, for often a little treatment or advice will help and prevent serious trouble, while if the disease gets well rooted, it is almost impossible to eradicate it. We need counsel and advice at the first, and by seeking it we will save time, strength, and money.

Also again, let us remember that patent advertised medicines are dangerous things, and that we must not be tempted to take what we do not know all about.

Selfishness is a trait we all dislike. We do not want to so consider " self " that we become selfish, but, friends, let us never feel it is selfish to think of the beautiful homes which our Heavenly Fat er has given us. They are His gifts and need care, and so let us consider these few hints, and the others which thought will bring to us. Let us realize that health cannot be bought, but it can be worked for, and that it is a possession that once lost is hard to recover. Strong, ·healthy, wise, let us go on to womanhood, with bodies prepared by no ill-use or forgetfulness to meet the strains which will come to us.

Faithfully your friend,

G. H. D.

SHOPPING—DRESS.

Dear Girls :

In this letter we come to a matter of very great importance to each one of us, and a subject which has interested womanhood during the past six thousand years. It is one we have to think of for our baby sisters, and again for our old grandmothers.

Since our mother Eve sewed fig-tree leaves together in the old garden of Eden, women have thought of, planned for, and sewed on garments of all sorts of shapes, styles, and material.

We girls work to get clothes, and are constantly planning how to cover the houses whose health we considered in our last letter.

It is hard to discuss a matter on which we all have such decided ideas, and please do not think me old-maidish or prudish if I give you some of mine.

Going shopping comes first. Let us make up

our minds just what we need, and then think of what our purses contain, and decide we will not go beyond this.

A list will be found useful, even if we have only a few things to get. It will pay to go to several shops to secure prices and ideas, but don't let us be tempted by bargains.

How often we have wasted smaller or larger amounts by the temptation of seeing such and such an article for " only thirty-nine cents," or another for " twenty-three cents," ribbon marked down, or " lace just given away" ! If the article is needed, buy it, but don't purchase to lie by, just because it is " so cheap."

Good materials pay. It is better to go without for a little until we can get something worth making up. Pay for what you get. A dress or coat bought on the instalment plan, or one for which a debt is incurred, is a very expensive and trouble-some garment. It is worn out before it is paid for, and then another is needed, and so the debt goes on. Shop underclothes are now the fashion, still we confess to one another that they wear badly, and are not worth the money. They seem

cheap, and are less troublesome than to make our
own when we are so tired and busy at night. Consider whether they do pay. If we must buy, do
not be tempted by edges and inserting of lace or
embroidery. The first or second washing will tear
these away, and ragged or torn drawers, chemises,
skirts will be the result. Tucks, plain hems, and
good muslin make a garment that will wear and
wash well. Unbleached muslin wears better than
the white, and after one or two washings the garment becomes as white as the other made originally
of white goods.

Keep account of what you spend, and realize that it
is as important to save pennies as dollars, for shortly
the cents will become a dollar, if care is taken.
Those of us who know how, can save much by cutting out and making our dresses as well as underclothes. The Queen of England had her daughters
taught dress-making, and to-day classes for this are
very popular. If possible, let us, too, learn to cut
out and fit not only dresses, but also underclothes.
Machines are cheap, and those of us who are preparing to become wives and mothers must learn to
use them.

There is another kind of sewing, however, and yet many of us to-day pride ourselves that we do not know which finger the thimble goes on, nor hardly how to thread a needle. Proud of it! Why, I should be ashamed of such a fact if it were true of me! The needle is one of the most powerful instruments a woman can use. Let us be proud rather that we are good seamstresses.

Hats and bonnets are most inexpensive if we can trim them ourselves. Millinery classes should be as popular as those of dress-making.

Now to the dress itself. Underclothes we have spoken of. A well-dressed woman is judged by her stockings, shoes, gloves, and undergarments more almost than by her dresses. A bride should be proud of showing plain, well-sewed piles of night-dresses, drawers, chemises, skirts, etc., especially if she can point to such and such as made by herself. Neat, clean, well-clothed underneath!—are we this? I do not mean have we ruffles, flounces, and embroideries, but rather plain, neat things. Have we ever calculated how much we spend on ribbons and flowers, and how much on underclothing? The result will surprise many a girl, as

it would surprise her to know how much she spends
monthly in candy and sweets.

Pins and safety-pins seem to many of our minds
made to save buttons. How often things go back
and forth to the wash minus buttons ! This is not
neat. Neither are holes nor tears pinned together.
The old proverb, " A stitch in time saves nine," is
ever new, and how often have we proved it so in
our own experience !

These clothes of ours must be loose. Girls often
ask, " Do corsets hurt us ?" My experience says,
" No," if perfectly loose. They should be so that
our hand can slip down them, and if we give a sigh
of relief when we take off our clothes and corsets at
night, we can be sure they are hurting us. Loosen
them. Oh, dear girl friends, do let us think ahead,
and feel that it is more important to be strong, happy
women than to have for a few years a *small* waist.
Such a waist must harm us. We will suffer for
the tight lacing, and if God ever grants us the
blessing of children, they, too, will suffer. Does it
pay ? The health clothing, where no corsets are
worn, but instead all are made to hang on loose
waists, is most valuable. I wish we could all wear

it ; but as it seems we cannot, let us see if, with
what we have, we can dress healthfully. Bands
should be loose, skirts as light as possible, and
again, above all, no tight lacing. Have you ever
weighed your Sunday dress skirt? Weigh it
some day, and see if you are not surprised by the
result.

There come now ladies' suspenders, and these are
invaluable, for they lift the skirt from bearing
down upon the stomach and back, and put the
weight on the shoulders. Strips of muslin (unbleached is stiffer) answer as well as bought suspenders. Take strips of double thickness, about
two inches wide, sew them on the band of your
dress at the back, and when you put it on, cross the
strips behind, and fasten them on to the front band
by means of buttons or safety-pins. Working dresses
should be specially light and loose.

A gentleman who is very particular, when asked
by a friend " what constitutes a well-dressed
lady," replied, " When you see her coming, you
should notice her face and herself, not her clothes.
Second. Her gloves and shoes must be whole and
clean." When urged, he explained farther, and

added, " A woman should be noticed for herself, not her clothes. Often a startling bow, feather, or even buttons will take from the dress of a woman, and it be noticed, not she herself." This gentleman may have an extreme idea, but, girls, there is truth in what he says. Surely we want ourselves noticed, not what is put on us.

Dress must be quiet, simple, and in harmony. I could hardly say what to buy, for seasons differ, and, still more, ideas vary. Let our dress be suitable for the occasion and for ourselves, and let us remember that a true, bright woman is never thought of for her clothes—that is, if they are neat —but rather for herself.

A gingham or plain woollen dress can make a girl look as charmingly as a silk, and for ordinary life would be much more suitable.

There are some health hints in the discussion of dress which must not be left out. One or two we have spoken of. Another relates to the foot-covering. High heels throw the body forward and put out of position almost every part of the body, the result often being injury to it, which, however, can hardly be recognized, it is of so slow a growth.

They affect the eyes so much that one of the first questions a leading oculist asks when one goes to consult him is, " Let me see your feet."

Then, thin soles for walking are very bad, as dampness must sift through, often bringing on lung weakness or a severe cold. Rubbers many a girl scorns. Why ? Simply because they make the feet look ugly, and are troublesome. Do let us be sensible, and not scorn such useful articles. If we are caught out in the rain, or if it comes on while we are at work and our feet are not prepared for the wet, let us arrange paper soles. Cut out pieces of brown or newspaper the size of your feet, and slip these soles in your boots. The paper will protect the feet wonderfully. If shoes have holes, do the same thing, and dampness and cold will be kept out for a long time. Paper is always useful for warmth. Men have lined coats with it. It has been used to make an extra blanket by many a poor person. Buy a morning paper, read it, and then keep it for a cold spell of weather, and thus make your news useful. Girls can tuck it inside of a thin coat, and for a few hours it will keep them warm and comfortable. Renew it, and so on. Be careful in the early spring against taking off flannels or winter things. It is better to suffer a few days than to run any risk.

And in the same direction, do not let us, from any feeling of pride or desire for looking well, take off and put on lighter and heavier wraps. Often a girl on Sunday will put on a thin jacket or garment, when all the week she had worn a heavy shawl or coat. Still oftener will she do this for some evening entertainment. Hundreds have died from lung trouble by such thoughtlessness.

This applies also to neck wraps, furs, etc. Our throats are better never wrapped up than having them exposed, then covered and exposed again. A little thing, but oh, how serious the consequence can be !

May I add just here, don't sit in damp, wet clothes. How often, for pleasure or pure thoughtlessness, we wait one, two, or more hours before changing skirts, shoes, and stockings after having been caught in the wet ! A chill or cold would seem a small result of such carelessness, but almost surely these will run into something worse. We girls cannot afford to say, " Oh, I forgot !" " I did not think !" "I thought it would make no difference."

All these things make differences, and we want to be true to ourselves and to others in every particular ; true also in this dress which protects and yet will beautify us if we will only let it.

Can we think of dress or the body-covering and not think of those words of St. Paul, " Our bodies are the temples of the Holy Ghost" ? Surely they are worth both being taken care of and of being well clothed. May we, as girls, feel that this means much more than the apparent style and quality of our things ; rather that thought and care will show us how, without spending more money, but rather brains and common-sense, we can be well clothed, meaning neatness, order, and becomingness in the sense meant by an English lady, who writes, " Becoming things are really things that suit you in size and fit, as well as color—not things of a fashion that may have been invented to suit some one as unlike you as possible."

Your true friend,

G. II. D.

MEN FRIENDS—PROSPECTIVE HUSBANDS AND WIVES.

SOME of you remember, dear friends, an evening three years ago, when in our small Fortieth Street room a large and jolly crowd of us were meeting. The rooms were full, and an eager look was on many faces. "What is going on?" asked an outsider. A member answered, "Oh, we are to discuss to-night how to select a husband, and other interesting things!" The outsider joined our numbers, and quickly we were all intently busy listening and talking. Fun and laughter soon died away, and an earnest, tender look came on many of our faces, for our subject lay so near home. Each girl was pondering that unknown future, and deep down in our hearts came new thoughts and resolutions.

If we were to be queens in a centre, if a new *home* or household was to be formed by us, how important it was to learn all we could of how to select a being or other head of the house ! Our life companion ! The one whom we would have to promise to love, honor, and obey.

The evening proved one long to be remembered by us all, and now, girls, in letter-form some of our ideas are to find shape.

There are few of us who are not glad to feel that we have some men friends ; some have more, some less. A few of these we have known always, having grown up with them ; others we have met from having known their sisters ; others have been introduced by mutual friends ; some others we have met, and it would be hard to know just when and where. Of these latter we know very little, and just here let us stop and ask ourselves whether it is wise to become intimate or " to keep company" with a man, either younger or older, whom we really could tell nothing about except that we had met him on the cars, street, or at our work. What can we know about such a one, and yet how many of us enjoy the fun of a talk or a walk with a man whom we have only just met ! I think that we should set too high a value upon ourselves to allow any such freedom, for the talk and walk will

unconsciously lead to others, and so on until we
feel that the young man is one of our friends ; and
yet what do we really know of him ? Nothing except he seems well dressed—that he is fun to talk
to. Do let us be careful and not form such intimacies, but determine that we will have no men
friends without having been introduced to them,
or know all about them.

It is pleasant to have men friends, yet there are
so many stamps of men, and we girls should be
anxious to secure for friends the nicest. I do not
mean the best dressed, but the truest and noblest
in themselves—manly men, who are not ashamed of
hard work, and who are glad of opportunities for
learning a trade, or beginning down at the bottom
and working their way up to high wages and hearty
esteem. Such men are rare, and yet, girls, let us
not be content with those men we meet so many
of, whose sole thought is present pleasure, clothes,
and self-indulgence. We may have to meet such,
but let it be only in an acquaintanceship way. We
girls and women certainly respect ourselves, yet
thoughtlessly we are in danger of allowing liberties, of wishing to attract attention, etc., in these

acquaintanceships of ours. Thus let us constantly be on our guard in this stage of friendship, as well as later.

Let us try, with our mother's help, to make ready some room at home—even a kitchen can be bright and cheery—where we can see our men friends. So often mothers are tired and discouraged, and think it all right for us to see our companions on the streets; but, girls, we need the protection of our own homes, however poor, and if we will only help our mother make ready, she will gladly in her turn aid us in cleaning up one room for company. There are dangers on the streets and at places of amusement which in another letter we will speak of.

By and by, when we are older (for surely none of us will be so foolish as to make a life decision before we are at least eighteen or nineteen), among all the men we meet there will be one we think of more often than of the others; we like him better and better, and suddenly we say to ourselves, "I have fallen in love; I am ready to give up all for one man." Dear friends, what does this mean? It should mean, I have studied this man, I have found out all about him, I thoroughly respect him.

Some person asks, " What have you found out ?
Why do you respect him ?"   " I know that he is
kind to his companions, and to his mother and sisters ; that he is good-tempered ; that he is not
found around saloons ; that he has steady work ; that
he has not many fine clothes, but rather a bank-
book and a good deposit to his credit.   I know
he takes books from a library, and is anxious to
rise ; also that on Sundays he goes to church, at
least once during the day ; that, farther, he is
thoughtful and kind to those not so well off as
himself, and does not run after many girls, but
rather has selected me to be to him his dearest
and best friend."

Girls, how many of us could thus answer ?   But
should we not know our prospective husband thoroughly well before marriage, if we want to be
happy afterward ;   know him in his working
clothes as well as in his Sunday ones ; know him at
his own home as well as abroad ?   We would take
care not to buy a dress in a hurry without knowing
what we got for our money, and yet girls often
choose a man and take him for a husband without
knowing him anywhere except on the street and in

his one suit of good clothes. Then, girl friends, don't let us speak lightly of marriage or falling in love ; it seems so dreadful to hear girls laughing and joking over what is to them the most solemn thing of life. *Pray* rather than laugh over these things.

Again, falling in love, if the love is on sure foundation, it is not a thing to be ashamed of. Our Heavenly Father Himself told us, " It is not good that man should be alone," and He has given us a longing for mutual love and sympathy. Love is a wondrous term, and yet we use it so carelessly and freely ! It really means self-sacrifice, thinking or caring so much for some one else that we feel no pain and care too great if we can save the loved one from the pain and care.

Respect and perfect confidence are at the root of all true love. This man we are thinking of giving ourselves to, do we respect him, or do we ourselves wish to pass over certain serious faults in him, such as a love for drink or gambling, a selfish nature, a careless way of talking of his home and mother, a fondness for loafing, a disregard for church, one who is constantly changing his work, etc. ? After a while we cannot pass over these faults, if we really give ourselves to him, for when the home life begins, the habits will be apt to get stronger, and sore sorrow and suffering will follow. Yes, it is most important to select the companion of life only after earnest thought and prayer.

Thousands of women could gather around us to-day and could bear testimony to this point. They could tell us how, when they were young, perhaps only sixteen, seventeen, or eighteen, they thought they fell in love, and hastily bound themselves to a man for life whom they really did not know, or what they did know was not very good. How soon these poor women regretted it, and how they have suffered since ; not they only, but also the children that came to them. Unhappy homes were the further consequences, and the poor women to-day are tired, utterly discouraged, and weak from long want and suffering.

Girls, how often do we realize that the man we are thinking of for our husband is also to be the father of our children ! Is he one we would want in this capacity ?

Motherhood and fatherhood are sacred terms,

and can we lightly enter into any relationship that may bring such responsibilities upon us ?

We are engaged ! keeping company has passed, and now we are preparing for the coming together. For this period, which is a happy one .o most couples, we cannot forbear giving a few hints. Perfect confidence and truthfulness must exist between the girl and man. Things will come to light sooner or later, and it is far better to be frank and tell about the past of both lives.

To keep a man's love you must keep his respect, and to keep that you must never pass the bounds of maidenly modesty and reserve, even with him. How often you hear a girl say, " Oh, it doesn't matter what I do or say, when we are going to be married !" It does matter, and until you are married you must not behave as if you were. A girl who allows a man, even the man she is engaged to, to take any liberties with her, or to fail in the politeness which every man owes to a woman, is not the girl to win and keep a man's respect.

His and your parents are both worthy of your consideration, and you should think of their comfort and care. Don't allow yourself flirtations or fun with other men. You are pledged to one, and cannot be too careful to keep his esteem. Don't tease him, therefore, by flirting.

And, girls, while we have been talking of the husband and the man, do we remember that we, too, have a part to play? Are we ready for the duties and responsibilities that must come to us? Do we try and make ready by learning all we can about the care that will soon be ours? Many claim that knowledge of housekeeping, cooking, etc., come by nature to a girl when she is married. Indeed they do not, as many a married girl would tell us. Knowledge brings power. Surely, knowing how to cook, how to care for our rooms, how to sew, how to keep accounts, how to market, must give us added power in making a happy home.

Many of us have to work hard up to the day of our marriage, but our friend will respect us more if we insist upon one or two evenings a week being given to study or work, which will give us skill in being good housewives. Our mothers can help us, and will probably gladly do so, or we can join classes by paying a small sum, such money being one of our best investments toward a happy home. Then we must prepare our clothes. Have good ginghams ready and aprons to work in. Have underclothing plain and easy to wash. Fussy things are put away as useless after a few weeks. Plan even to have the wedding dress suitable for some use afterward. Some store of sheets, blankets, and table-linen will be more valuable than extra dresses, even if they do not apparently make as much show. We must try and arrange to be thoroughly well at the date of our marriage, and do not let this be a secret one. A new life started out in any sort of deceit cannot be a happy one.

Sweetheart is a term we often use, and as a close to our letter I want to give you a definition of the word written by a lady far away. She was speaking to a group of girls on just our subject, under the title of "Sweethearts," and ends her thoughts with these words : "Ah ! dear girls, I wish I could set before you the picture of what a true maiden should be : so gentle and loving, so pure and modest, not seeking, but being sought ; found out, like the violet among the leaves, rather by her sweetness than her beauty—a maiden of

whom all good men would say, ' That is a woman
I could love and honor as my wife—a woman I
could trust with the happiness of my home and
the bringing up of my children ! ' Such a maiden
would indeed be herself a ' *sweetheart* ' whom a
man could love and respect."

Earnestly wishing that the above can be said
about each one of us, I remain, dear sister friends,

Very faithfully,

G. H. D.

HOME LIFE.

Dear Girls :

Home ! Husband ! Wife ! Mother ! Father ! Brothers ! Sisters ! What words these are to many of us, representing the place that is so dear and the beings that make our family ties !

Family life nowadays is not always as happy as it should be. We want to stop and think what the above words really mean.

Here is a kingdom or little world by itself, containing within four walls from two to eight or ten human lives connected closely together. The heads we have already thought of, and now want to only add that, as the *heads*, they must be the rulers, and together lay down certain rules and plans which should be followed out if there is to be harmony and regular living. A home should be the brightest, happiest place in the world to the inmates, where not only sympathy and love may be found, but where also all may know that on returning to it there will be cheer and sympathy—such things as the prompt serving of meals, having the rooms in order at certain hours, little things done each for the other, which show consideration and care.

Let us ask ourselves two plain questions, and thoughtfully consider them before answering : Are our homes all they ought to be ? Are there not some ways in which even we can contribute to make them better—I mean happier, and more like our ideas of a home ?

Women, young and old, have such responsibilities here ! Do not throw them off, but take up the burdens with brave cheerfulness. Mothers and daughters are often not the friends they should be. Dozens of girls will come and tell me things as their friend who will not think of talking the matters over with their mothers. These love their girls, but have not taught them to come in confidence to them.

Daughters, do you realize what your mothers did for you ? How for weeks and months they suffered discomfort and often pain for you ? How there came hours of agony, and then, as a little

helpless creature, they looked after your wants ?
How they guided and protected you as a young
child ? How many nights, do you suppose, has your
mother walked the floor with you ? How many
hours of anxiety have been passed by your sick-
bed ? How many stitches have been put in clothes
for you ? I am sure many millions ; for you they
have worked and suffered, and yet as you get older
and they venture to warn and counsel you, the
thought is, " Oh, it's only mother !" " She's always bothering about something or other !" " I
don't care, it's only mother again," when you want
to go off and leave to the home care-taker duties
that you should do.

Only mother ! How her heart must ache when
she feels that mother is the last person her daughter pays any heed to ! It should be mother and
father above all others. They should be our truest
friends. " But mother is so cross and unreasonable," you say ; " she forgets what fun is." You,
too, would be apt to be cross and unreasonable if
your body had suffered as much as your mother's
has for you ; and if only you would show her more
love and care, you would get in return more of

the affection that she showed you when you were a little child, for it is all there for you.

Jehovah on Mount Sinai, thousands of years ago, gave as one of His ten commands the words, "Honor thy father and mother." One of our catechisms says, "We should love, honor, and succor our parents." Oh, girls, which one of us does this as we should ? Obey is not put here, for how can we love and honor without obedience ? As we become fourteen, fifteen, and over we feel ourselves very old, and much too old to think of mother's wishes.

George Washington, who is known and revered all over this country as the saviour of his country, felt it his duty and pleasure to go to the home where sat his aged mother and pay her honor and respect. He was not too old to obey that mother.

It may be that we girls feel it makes no difference how we look when no company is coming in. I think some fathers would hardly know their girls without curl-papers and a shabby dress. We keep the dressing-up for company. Necessarily there must be best dresses laid by for special occasions, but is that any reason why we should not look neatly and pretty for our fathers and brothers ? Don't save for them all the old rags and tags, but let them see when they come home at night-time wife and daughter in perhaps only fresh gingham or calico dress, but with collars or ruffles on, and hair out of papers. Some of you have acknowledged to me that "of course you always wear curl-papers at home." They are taken off when company manners are put on.

The true lady will be as courteous, polite, and kind at home as in company. How often do we remember "thank you," "please," "excuse me," at home ? Should not brothers, sisters, and parents hear these words as well as strangers ?

How many of us think of meal-times only as occasions for swallowing down food, and then rushing off to work or pleasure ? Let us in the home life try to make at least the evening meal a time for mutual interest, telling one another in the family things which have happened during the day, and seeing if this time cannot be made ' .ight and happy.

Do you have sunshine in your rooms ? "No," you say, "but I wish we had it." "Why not get some ?" "How ?" "Why, by shining your-selves."

Smiles and a bright face will lighten a room as sunshine. In the morning it is hard to be sun-beams, and yet we must be these or clouds. A cross, gloomy face will darken a whole room, and the cloud will stay all day.

Sisters can have wonderful influence over broth-ers. Is it on the true side ? Do we sympathize and care for the boys ? "Tom is such a bother ;" "Jack is the greatest plague of my life ;" "I never saw such a boy ;" "I wish you would clear out, I am busy ;" "Don't disturb me"—these are expressions brothers often hear from their home womenkind. Have the sisters tried to help Tom, and to interest him in something ? Do you won-der Jack is a plague, when he has never been treated with love or consideration ? Don't be al-ways interested in other girls' brothers, but do care and think sometimes for your own. Helpful, lov-ing sisters, who will not mind giving up an evening to the amusement of the boy brother, who will be ready to mend for him the kite or balls, who will be interested in his concerns, are rare, yet they are

found, and are bright examples for the rest of us.
The little children need us, and we all know how
we can comfort and amuse them, as well as save
our mother's tired back and fingers by caring and
sewing for them.

The grandmothers or other aged members of the
home circle need our loving thought. They may
seem very unreasonable and troublesome, may be
old-fashioned and queer, but their age should command respect, and we young people should be only
proud if we can show it to them.

Try and make home attractive by not only care
and neatness, but also by work and thought. There
are many little things that can be made from very
little, and that will cost very little. Common bur-
laps, with bright flannels or calico, make many
things. Ingenuity can turn an old barrel into a
pretty chintz seat. Pressed leaves and flowers ar-
ranged tastefully, plants growing in a common box,
bring a bright look into many a home. A lamp
burning handy for reading or sewing, some books
from the circulating library, a paper bought which
will entertain the family, will often bring an interest
into an evening, and if one member of the family

will try reading aloud it is wonderful how bright it will make the children, and how it will amuse them.

The streets are such dreadful places to find amusement in, and yet they are only too attractive to us all. Try and create or bring some attraction into our own rooms, so that not only we but the rest may find them pleasant.

An object in life means that there is a thing that is earnestly sought after or striven for. Every one of us should have for our first object in our own lives an earnest desire to serve our Heavenly Father, and our second should be to serve others. Nowhere could we have a better place to practise our second object than in our homes. Who among us after this talk will strive to make home as bright and attractive as possible ? Who will strive to forget self in thinking of making father, mother, brothers, and sisters happy ?

"I am only one of a large family," I hear one of the girls say. "I am at work all day and get home so tired," another answers. "I have no knack," a third thinks. "It all seems so hopeless, I don't see the use of trying," comes from still another. I know it all, dear fellow-girls ; I have been through with many of your thoughts, but I will not let any of us become too discouraged.

The one member probably cannot immediately create a revolution, but the one can do some little thing as a starting point, and can suggest others. She, by making the best of what she has, can often start other members thinking, and gradually the small ray will shine among all the rest. The busy working girl who gets so tired cannot be expected to do much of the household work, but she can feel that by her labor she is helping on the home life, and then mornings and evenings and Sundays she can take bright, cheery views of matters in general and home matters in particular.

She can bring pleasant words with her rather than cross, scolding ones. She can try and tell something she has seen or heard, and in numberless ways bring in brightness and cheer.

You, hopeless friend, look up! Nothing is hopeless in this world. Even in your dark, cheerless room, with no extra money, no apparent harmony, cheer and gladness can gradually come if each one of you will do your best to make the best of what you have.

Start to do so first, and keep on trying until you will see some improvement ; more will follow.

You have known that by one victory you may often secure another, so don't give up looking out for some means of bringing in sunshine, even if you are small, young, and apparently hedged in by many discouragements.

> " Home, sweet home,
> There's no place like home,"

is a refrain we all love to sing. Oh, girls, will you not try to make your homes so pleasant that they will be happy memories in the family life, and places where so much sweetness and good are found that they will truly be homes in which to fit us for that Eternal Home which is making ready for each one who will earnestly live toward it, trusting wholly in that Maker who Himself knows the difficulties of the home life here, and who will help each one who trusts in Him !

Faithfully yours,

G. H. D.

HOUSEKEEPING SUGGESTIONS.

DEAR GIRLS :

Let us again take a peep into home life to-day, and discuss some matters there. We have had our thoughts upon prospective husbands and wives, upon homes, and now come to the starting of and working in homes. This may mean with a husband, and we as the wife, with much responsibility, or it may be as a daughter, who has to aid in finding for her family a home circle.

In large cities it is a hard problem to know how to find suitable rooms or houses. Everything is crowded, and our large tenements do not make attractive dwellings ; still in them there are many happy homes, and we have all the opportunity of creating another.

In moving into or in selecting rooms, try and find a place where the sun will shine at least half of the day, and where drafts through the rooms can be obtained. Stairs are hard to climb, but if we are at all strong, it will be worth the effort to be up two or three flights, for the air is purer higher up. Sunlight and air are the best disinfectants, and are needed if we are to have healthy homes.

The rooms must be thoroughly clean. White-wash and cheap wall papers, which we can put on ourselves, cost little, and at the outset they will give the home a fresh look.

Now the furniture. If we already have this, care is only needed to make it go as far as possible in the new places, or to economize space, so that much can go where little is needed.

If furniture has to be bought, do try and only get what you can pay for. A debt is a trouble-some thing to carry into the new quarters. Buy-ing on the instalment plan has ruined many a young couple.

Make the kitchen or living-room your first thought ; then the bedrooms ; and when you have fully equipped these, what money is left can go into the parlor.

Useful things before show should be the rule. I have known of girls who had a fine set of furniture in the front room and a flowery carpet, but in the kitchen was hardly a tin or pan, no serviceable china or other necessary articles.

A kitchen can be made one of the pleasantest places imaginable, with shining tins on the walls, well-blackened stove, white and yellow china on shelves where pretty scalloped paper covers the edges, pots and kettles hidden in a closet, oil-cloth on the floor, a thinner piece for a cover on the table, when it is not in use.

But we are not going into the further mysteries of furnishing in this short letter, but rather are to step into the rooms furnished, and are to talk over some simple housekeeping questions. First, as to one of the greatest difficulties of the modern flat or floor—namely, lack of space to put the numerous things that must accumulate, the scarcity of dress closet room, and such other complications.

Once start out with confusion, and it will seem hard ever to create order. It is absolutely necessary to keep things in order, and to do so some things must be invented. Bags will be found useful. An old calico dress skirt (where the waist is faded or worn out) cut into strips will make several bags.

Have two or three for soiled clothes, and try to throw into them distinct kinds of things, so as to save trouble on wash-day. Thus in one put the small pieces, as collars, cuffs, handkerchiefs, and in another the skirts and underclothes. These bags should hang on a heavy nail behind the door.

Another of different size and color can hold pieces of dress goods, etc. Smaller bags hold the small bits, only too often thrown away.

A soap-box neatly covered with dark muslin or paper and put in a corner or even under the bed will hold spare shoes and rubbers of different members of the family, which look so badly lying around.

A trunk in the corner, with its chintz cover, can contain summer or winter dresses in their turn neatly folded. Here, too, will go some valued possession, and care should be taken to have it always securely locked.

If dresses have to hang in the room, be sure and have a curtain of muslin or calico to hang before them, both for looks and to keep them from the dust.

In the kitchen one or more covered boxes will

again be found useful ; in one lay the kindlings and bits of paper, in another odds and ends that necessarily will gather together.

If we can afford a small wicker basket for scraps of paper, etc., it will be well ; if not, make a scrap-basket of a smaller box. A receptacle for these bits is invaluable. "A place for everything and everything in its place," is an adage well worth the remembering.

Bureau-drawers have a great faculty of never being in order. How often have we gone through one in a hurry, and have turned the whole contents upside down before we have found what we wanted ; then have rushed off, saying, " Oh, I will fix it later !" When does *later* come ? I have myself done this so often, and I imagine you have, too.

Now I try to check myself, and stop a moment to put the things back one by one as I search through them, and find it much less trouble.

Here are three good suggestions to learn and remember : A place for everything, even odds and ends. Put away everything as we use it. "Could I find it in the dark again ?"

This last seems funny, but do you know why we

have to rummage so often ? It is because we forget where we put things. If we keep in mind looking for a thing in the dark, and try to think of where things go, we could say with a young girl I know of, "I think I could find everything of mine, even if I suddenly became blind."

Another word as to drawers : Do try to keep out of them everything that could possibly be anywhere else. Thus we find drawers full of a variety of things that could be put in the top tray of a trunk, because for a few months they are not to be used. Pieces of rags, bits of fruit or candy, old newspapers, scraps, etc., accumulate in a top drawer, until it comes to look like a small boy's pocket. It seems very hard to keep it in order, for into it pops everything that should be got out of the way, or for which we do not know where to find a place. Is not this true ?

Our bedrooms are the places where we sleep, where we spend those valuable hours of rest which are needed to fit us for work. It is difficult to make these airy in modern houses, so they must be kept as free as possible from impurities. Never leave in them flowers, fruits, or other vegetable matter at night. Try and keep them clean and free from dust. Do not let laziness keep you from carrying out the slops as soon as possible. Let the bed air at least an hour, and even in winter do not be afraid to open windows in the room or in the living-room, and let the air through. In February and March the beds should have thorough cleaning with salted soap-suds, and afterward must be powdered.

Washing is a hard task where water has to be carried, but all our work is hard. Let us remember that labor saved now often results in double the work later; so try and wash frequently, and not let in our small rooms soiled clothes accumulate.

Again, on account of the hardness of washing, do not let us feel we can keep on dirty things, even when they are not seen. I have somewhere read " that a tidy mother often makes an untidy daughter." Why should this be? Because if the mother is always ready to step in and pick up after us, or to keep order, we daughters are apt to let her. This should not be so. We are stronger than our mothers, and surely we will not let her goodness be imposed upon.

A word to mothers. Is it not your fault that your girls are careless and heedless? You should from early days make them careful.

The kitchen is an important element in every home. The fire needs attention first, and we can give it only a word, and that is, use brains and care over it. Have ready, the wood, paper, and coal the night before. Think of it often, and, above all else, don't use kerosene for lighting it because you are in a hurry. Many lives and homes are lost by the free use of kerosene, and don't let us furnish a good paragraph in the newspapers, as well as much sorrow to other people, by our laziness.

Refrigerators want thorough washing at least once a week with borax and water, and need to be well dried. The blanket used on the ice should be dried frequently and washed occasionally. A little charcoal standing in a saucer amid the food purifies. Tainted food is most harmful. Do be careful, therefore, of the refrigerator.

Tables and woodenware should be washed with cold water and sand ; also the floors. Soles of men's old boots make scrubbing-brushes when we find it hard to afford sufficient.

Hooks are useful in kitchens, for on them can be hung much that it is hard to find place for. Be careful not to accumulate here what is not needed, and to keep order.

In ordinary flats or sets of rooms, plumbing or water is only introduced into the kitchen. Too much care cannot be taken here. No refuse must stop the drain-pipe in the sink. Fresh water must often be allowed to run down, and at intervals it is wise to throw some disinfectant. Chlorate of lime dissolved in hot water is not very costly and it will keep pipes healthy.

Little need be said about the living-room, for here care is usually exercised. Only a few general points need be added. If one has to leave dirt in the room when sweeping, leave it in the middle of the floor, for then people will know it is there for a purpose, and not out of carelessness. Dust under sofas, chairs, or in corners suggests poor house-cleaning.

Work, if possible, with system, planning out duties as far as possible with method, and try and have regular days for regular duties. Don't hurry, take things as they come from day to day, and try not to look ahead.

Put heart into even dish-washing, and see if it does not come easier. Sing about your work; it will lighten it. Do always the best you can, and then leave the rest; but be sure the best is first done.

Patience is needed, and previous training. Now when we are younger, and specially if we are still in our mother's home, make preparation for the house duties.

Truly your friend,

G. H. D.

MARKETING AND FOOD.

DEAR FRIENDS :

How often I have heard the expression, " Oh, I wish I could get along without eating !" It is a vain wish, for we all have to eat. Food is of vital importance, necessary to every creature with life. It gives occupation also to thousands of men and women, and from this necessity of our living come much of the world's commerce and business.

It affects us in all sorts of surprising ways. Being of such importance, it sometimes seems strange that it does not influence our thoughts more. There are children and grown people, too, who seem to live simply to eat or drink. It is their one thought—a thought, however, based upon a gluttonous selfishness, and not upon the idea of food as a means of bringing strength and nutriment to the body, fitting it for earnest, helpful work.

Women have generally to think of the food question more than men, for to them comes the neces-

sity of furnishing and preparing the household
meals.

They are the care-takers, and one of their principal cares comes from thinking, "What shall I
give them to eat?" Often the wonderment comes
just before twelve or six o'clock, and is caused by
no thought having been taken on the matter before.

Among the ways of bringing comfort and harmony into a home, there are few more necessary
than the thinking of and preparing for meals, so that
they are always promptly served hot and appetizing. These results do not come by chance, nor
will they be in our house if the care-taker thinks
of them in a hap-hazard way, not realizing their
importance.

We girls, in our talks upon the future home-keep-
ing, must not therefore forget the food question.

A kitchen utensil called a sieve we are all familiar with. I trust, however, that we are not so
familiar with it that we imitate its action. It is
used in many ways, but all with the same object
in view—namely, that of sifting out or separating
the good fine substance from the coarser or uneat-
able matter.

Now, I have known people like sieves, for much
of the advice, many of the good ideas which come
to them in their life either from friends, teachers,
or from books, seem to sift through them, and only
the dregs are left behind—"In one ear and out
the other." Let us be pails or solid boxes, and
keep these talks safe in the brain ; only bring out
the hints or ideas when they can tell upon or influence our lives.

Thus with food : take in the hints we are to talk
of, and bring them out at home and elsewhere,
where their practice will do good.

Buying food, or marketing, is the first consideration. Here we can apply the rules we h a given
for shopping and also others. Make up a list men-
tally or on paper of just what you need. Calculate
ahead, and decide as to just how much money you
can spend for food in your week's allowance.
Thus on Monday morning do not go and give a
dollar for that day's meals, seventy-five cents the
next day, and by the end of the week find that
your family must starve, or that you must borrow,
or that you must run in debt.

It is well to set aside on Monday what you can

spend on the table during the week ; then determine
how judiciously you can spend it, so as to give
equally good meals during the next six or seven
days.   In this thought old accounts will be found
useful.

When moving into a new neighborhood inquire
around, or try several until you can select the best
butcher and grocer.   Deal then regularly with the
same, for you will be treated better as being a regular customer than if you were known to run around
trying experiments with tradespeople.

Do try *cash payments*.   Monthly house bills
have brought many a heartache and quarrel into
homes.

The cheapest kinds of food are sometimes the
most wholesome and strengthening, but in order to
utilize we must know how to choose them for their
freshness, goodness, and suitability to our needs.
There are tests for buying meat and vegetables,
etc., but here we cannot go into them.

Let me urge you, however, to learn these tests
before you set up housekeeping for yourselves, for
they will be wonderful helps.   I will also add that
I hope you will learn in some cooking class how to

use cheap cuts of beef and mutton ; how to make
soups out of scraps ; how to use over old pieces,
etc. The French are known all over the world as
wonderful cooks. Their tables are always good,
and it is a pleasure to be invited to dine where a
French person has prepared the meal. They are
also the most economical. Why ? Simply because
they know how to use scraps and cold bits so well,
and how to buy for little money a variety of odds
and ends which, when well served, make good, nourishing food.

Their pot-au-feu I wish we could copy. It is an
iron pot, either larger or smaller, and into it are
thrown all sorts of bits which ordinary cooks would
throw into the swill-pail. Bones, trimmings cut
from meat, ends of vegetables, potato-peelings,
broken pieces of bread, etc.—these are kept constantly boiling in water, and from this pot are manufactured all kinds of delicious soups and sauces.

Cooking classes will teach us of these and other
matters. Don't let us ask of the teacher, as some
girls I knew once demanded, only to make des-
serts, salads, cakes, etc. Let us rather learn how
to broil, not to waste, bread-making, soups, differ-

ent ways of serving eggs, potatoes, and cold bits,
etc. These mastered, we can easily pick up the
luxuries of eating afterward.

Besides being economical in cooking, there are
three other essentials which we should early know.
First. Perfect cleanliness—cleanliness of the person, of the utensils, and in the preparation of the
food. Second. System or regular method. This
is the power of doing work in such a way that one
result follows another in a quiet, orderly manner.
Lastly, accuracy. When a receipt has been proved
good, it should be followed exactly. Carelessness in
measuring is often the cause of failure.

But to go back to our subject. A mixed diet is
the best. Our bodies are made up of different
tissues. Each needs its proper food, and no one
kind contains all the elements we need. Therefore,
a diet composed of meat and vegetables in proper
quantities is considered the best.

Meat enriches the blood and tends to give us firm-
ness of muscle and general strength. This is more
needed in winter than in summer.

Fats should not be avoided entirely, as they furnish the best fuel for heating the body. Butter is

good for us if not eaten in too great quantities. Fish when fresh is an excellent article of food. Eggs are very nutritious. Hard-boiled, they are easily digested, and are useful for lunches. Vegetables and fruits are enjoyable and are wise provisions, as they furnish certain acids necessary to keep us in good working order.

If I speak of oatmeal, hominy, or other grains, I hear you girls say, " Oh, I hate these things !" or, " I can't eat such food." I don't wonder you do not like it, for few of you know how to prepare it. Well cooked—and to do this care and knowledge alone are necessary—these grains furnish cheap and very wholesome breakfasts or suppers. I cannot urge you too strongly to first learn how to cook, and then to freely use oatmeal and hominy. Black beans are another article that few of you know, yet these are life-supporting, and cost almost nothing. They make admirable soups.

I have known of ladies living for months on only dry bread and a variety of dried beans. They were students and had not means, so found that, by *knowing how*, they could keep well and strong on food costing only fifty cents per week, or seven cents per day.

Breads are wholesome if not eaten hot. Sweets I need not surely speak of ; you know all about them, even to the fact that they must not be too freely indulged in.

Milk is the most nourishing of drinks, and is much used in sickness. If it does not agree with you, try a little lime-water in it. Ice-water is dangerous if taken freely in hot weather. It should be drunk slowly, swallow by swallow, so as to prevent a sudden chill to the digestion. Small bits of ice held in the mouth will refresh and not harm, as too much ice-water does.

Tea and coffee in moderation help the nerves, but indulged largely in render us nervous. Cocoa and similar mixtures are nourishing, and will give variety to a supper. If a thing regularly disagrees with you, don't eat it.

One of the saddest sights in the world to me is that of a drunken woman, or one a victim of opium in some form. They have lost self-respect, modesty, and all that goes to make a true woman. Many that I have seen are very young ; they were girls only a short time before—girls like you and me.

Some of these girls, for the fun of it, took some stimulant ; it excited, rested, and helped them. A time came when they were tired or discouraged, and a glass of wine, a little gin and water was near them ; they took it, and the effect was such that they were again tempted. Easier and easier it grew, until all sense of the disgrace left them, or, if they felt it, they could not resist.

Other women in times of great pain went to doctors or friends who prescribed opium in some form. Such instant relief came, such a pleasurable sensation followed, that the desire grew to take " this delightful medicine." It was again and again taken.

The girl never thought of the harm, " for it was medicine, you know," she said. Medicine, yes ! most valuable for rare occasions, but constantly used the harmful results cannot be too strongly brought forward. Moral sense is soon lost, and misery for themselves and others the sure result.

Oh, girl friends, be warned ! There started some twelve or more years ago in a small Ohio town an association of a few earnest women. To-day that band numbers over three hundred thousand, scattered all over the country, with State, county, and city branches all under one earnest woman's brave leadership. These girls and women wear tiny blue or white ribbons, and are known as the National Women's Temperance Union. They are bound to a pledge of total abstinence, and can teach us many lessons of strong fighting for what is right and good. Such women you admire and are proud of. The others, weakened from yielding to intemperance and sin, you loathe.

These pictures came naturally into this talk on food and drinks. Will you think of them?

We come to the second part, the first having been, What shall we eat? and now a word as to *when* shall we eat.

Try to have regular hours for meals, and keep to these. The practice of eating now at one hour, now at another, is all wrong, for it gets the digestion into bad habits, which should work regularly, and have rests between.

Nibblers are great abusers of themselves, as we have already seen. Imagine how vexed and fretted the systematic, orderly stomach gets over the messes that nibblers constantly send into it, keeping it always worried, yet never properly at work!

Try not to do any work before eating in the morning. The one who has to prepare breakfast for the rest should eat a piece of bread and drink a little tea or milk before commencing her duties. Many a headache would be saved a tired housekeeper by this habit, and there would be fewer cross mothers or sisters at breakfast, if some little thing had been taken early in the morning.

Digestion does not progress well during sleep, so if anything has to be taken late in the evening, let it be something light and easy to digest.

Another caution : do not go to bed hungry. A glass of milk or piece of bread at this hour are helpful.

We have spoken of what and when to eat and drink, and now only a few words more as to how to eat.

Try to eat no more food than you have time to eat properly. Thought and study are needed to make a variety in our food, and they are also required in trying to set a pleasant table.

Food, however good and abundant, thrown on a table upon which there is no table-cloth, or one stained and mussy, with no order in the arrangement of dishes and plates, is not appetizing.

Again, one or two dishes of plain, simple things neatly and attractively served will taste and satisfy better than the former.

Let us try our woman's wit on the table, and see if we cannot make our meals pleasanter. The suggestion was given in another talk, but it is worthy of constant repetition, and not of repetition only, but also of being carried out.

Faithfully your friend,

G. H. D.

CARE OF THE SICK—EMERGENCIES.

DEAR GIRLS :

Sickness in the house brings to us not only anxiety and sorrow, but also many extra cares and responsibilities.

Love, unselfishness, and the giving of ourselves to the need of the sick person is seen, but often, with all the love and unselfishness, there is no comfort or relief to either nurses or patient during long weeks of pain and weakness. Why ? Because with all good desires and anxiety to do, no one in the home knows how to care for the sick member, and by the not knowing, she or he is subjected to many discomforts and annoyances which could be saved by tact and skill.

Books have been written on this subject, and it takes from one to two years of training before a woman is considered fitted to go out as a professional sick nurse.

Few of us will probably wish to give this time to

prepare ourselves, and fewer still wish to have this as their life's profession. All of us, however, must at times come into contact with sickness, and here are a few points which we can easily think of, and by practising them we may be better nurses or sick-room helpers.

Let the sick-room be the brightest and airiest on the floor, and endeavor to place the bed so that the window or door can be open without a draft upon it. Opening the former from the top is better than from the bottom. Doctors tell us that " each person spoils a gallon of air every minute," so quickly a roomful of pure air becomes impure.

If fresh air is necessary for those of us who are well, how much more important it is for those who are sick !

After pure air comes cleanliness. Everything about the bed and room must be kept clean and sweet. The patient herself must be frequently bathed and her clothing changed. Washing or bathing a sick person requires great care, for the slightest carelessness may bring on cold or a relapse.

Cold water should not be used without the doctor's orders ; rather warm water, with which mix a little alcohol. The person must never be entirely uncovered, except just that portion which is being washed, using some old shawl or blanket to wrap the rest of the body. Under her lay a rubber sheet or old blanket to prevent any danger from wetting the bed or bedding.

The bed itself needs constant care. It should be kept smooth and free from any crumbs or wrinkles. It is often a good plan to sew tapes on the lower sheet and tie it down tightly to the bed-posts. To change the sheets, one must roll up the soiled sheet lengthwise half way across the bed, and arrange the clean one smoothly on the empty space ; then lift or move the patient to the clean sheet, slip off the soiled one and spread out the clean, tucking it well in at the corners.

If a person is very sick it is well to give a little nourishment before the fatigue of changing the bedding. Sleep should be held almost sacred, and every care should be taken to prevent a sick person's being waked when once asleep—that is, without the doctor gives special directions about having her disturbed to receive nourishment. This latter point will tax our thoughts and care.

Cooking for the sick is an art in itself, and one which I hope you will all know something about; for a patient's food is often more important than his medicines.

Don't ever ask a sick person what she wants to eat. Let the food be unexpected, and served in an attractive way. Try and keep all idea of eating out of sight and mind except when the nourishment or meal must be given. Bring a little in at a time, and it will probably be found that the food must be given frequently. Surprises are often most pleasing, and they especially are enjoyed by a sick person when they come in the shape of some unexpected dainty or dish. A flower laid on the tray will interest and make her forget how disagreeable it is to eat, or some new style of cut or plate will attract attention and serve the same purpose. Try above all to bring nothing greasy to a patient, nor have on the tray any spotted napkin or cloth.

When you were once sick, do you remember how dreadful it was to hear a door creak, to have a person come into the room with noisy boots on? Do you not also remember how trying it was to have the doctor go out on the landing, and then have

him followed by your mother or sister ? You used
to hear them whispering there, and knew it was
about yourself. Then, when your care-taker came
back and you asked what they were saying, how
the answer used to be, " Oh, nothing of any importance." You would lie and toss and wonder
about it, and yet you were too tired to do so.
Then how you hated to have any one sit on your
bed, how you got cross and impatient over the slow
way of moving around your mother had, and how
you wished she would wear some dress that did not
rustle so. Such remembrances will do you good
when you come to take care of your sick friend or
relative. You should then know that unnecessary
noises, though slight, disturb a patient more than
louder noises, that are necessary. You will try and
have your door hinges well oiled, use old soft shoes,
have your calico without starch. You will work
quickly yet quietly.

If only you can have besides perception, or the
power of seeing what can be done and what cannot,
you will be a good nurse.

The same quality will be further needed, for you
must perceive constantly the condition of your

charge, and must keep careful note of the same, so as to be able to tell the doctor exactly what has occurred since he was last there. Don't have false modesty in talking with him, but tell him about every little point.

You must also obey his smallest directions. If he leaves many, I would advise writing them down, so that none need be overlooked.

There are several other little things which annoy a patient, and which we should try to avoid. Sweeping and hasty dusting are among these. A damp cloth put over a broom will prevent noise and the making of much dust, and a cloth should be used for the dusting, not a brush.

A table, covered with a fresh towel, should be behind the bed, and on this, medicine bottles and such things should be kept.

A bed-rest can be made from a small chair ; lean this on the top of its back, the seat also touching the bed. A good slant will be secured to cover with pillows. Make a pretty flannel jacket to slip on the patient when she sits up, rather than trying to wrap her in shawls.

As a nurse you will need much patience, and must

realize that your friend or charge is not accountable for crossness and extreme unreasonableness. Having so much extra work, you must care for yourself. It will not pay to go without sleep. Hearty meals must be taken, and extra nourishment. Farther, a bath daily when possible. Let the nurse get sick, the patient will be made worse, and more trouble will come into the home.

As visitors we will have to go and see many sick persons, and there are ideas here which, if followed, will make us welcome guests. Enter with a cheery, happy word. Don't exclaim, "Oh, how sick you look!" or, "How thin you have become!" Rather try and see some good point in the friend's condition, and refer to that. In your talk keep out all disagreeable remembrances, and tell no bad news. Don't stay long. If you ever are able to read to a sick friend, select a short story, and one without much excitement.

If you know how to make any nice little dish, make it as a surprise for the sick, but don't bring to her too much fruit or many sweets, and before bringing any find out if the doctor will allow them to be taken ; otherwise they will be only aggravations.

In case of visiting a person with a contagious disease, care must be taken not to go into the room without removing outer clothing, or, if possible, wearing a dress which can be washed. On leaving it one should bathe carefully and remove the clothing soon, especially before going among children. As nurses and visitors too much care cannot be exercised to prevent any spread of the contagion. Doing otherwise may mean innocent murder.

Accidents are constantly occurring. Emergencies come to us, and we must act in them. Strangely, the very first mode of acting must be the keeping cool, quiet, and collected ; ready to help, but if there is nothing that can be done except by the one or two, keeping out of the way of these.

In all accidents the poor person who has met with it must first be given plenty of air, and, secondly, he or she must be kept as quiet and free from excitement as possible. Thirdly, clothing must be loosened.

Think back and see how you all acted the last time there was an accident in the shop, and see which girl you wish to copy. We want to be true women, who are not made foolishly curious, neither

frightened out of all sense and reason by any accident or sudden danger. There is nothing to be
frightened at, and we must learn to help by keeping our own feelings under control.

If in the place where you work there are apt to
be accidents, it is well to have ready a few things—
some rolls of old muslin, pins, scisso᾽ , a bottle of
spirits of ammonia, and other simple remedies. A
few drops of spirits of ammonia in a half glass
of water revives any weakened person ; especially
where faintness comes will it be found helpful.
This can be used instead of brandy.

Simple fresh water is also invaluable to give as
drink or to sprinkle on the face. Don't, however,
throw it carelessly over a person. Many a one has
died of pneumonia instead of from the effects of
the accident, for some kind friend had thoroughly
wet their clothes by throwing water on them, and
these were not removed before cold had been taken,
which settled in pneumonia.

Blood is apt to startle both the injured person
and also those around. It should not, however,
for it is the natural result of many accidents. Blood,
however, must not be allowed to flow. It should be

stopped immediately. To do this, a clot of blood must be formed by forcing a continuous pressure on the wound. If it is small, your thumb will be found the quickest and handiest. If it is serious, something must be tied about the limb above the wound— that is, between it and the heart. Raise the limb also, and make the pressure tighter by putting a stick of any kind under the knot of the bandage, and twisting it several times. Put broken ice on a cloth and place it on the wound, for by making the blood cold it will more quickly clot.

Bear in mind this thing : don't take up the thumb or remove the bandage out of impatience or curiosity to see if the bleeding has stopped. Much harm may be done in this way. But if a doctor does not arrive, or if you are depending on yourselves altogether, then, when some time has passed, and you find that the blood has really ceased to flow, you may wash the wound gently by a stream of tepid water from a sponge, to remove any particles which should not be there. Then draw the wound carefully together, and put on narrow strips of adhesive plaster.

The first action required when a person is seen

on fire is to pick up instantly some rug, blanket, or woollen garment and envelop them, throwing it on the head or shoulders first, and then wrapping it around the body. This is done to prevent smoke or fire getting to the mouth. Burns and scalds must be kept free from air, and be well covered. White of an egg, pure linseed oil, the lather from a shaving-cup will quiet the pain, and then by wrapping the burn in linen or old muslin, this again in flannel or cotton batting, all danger of air further inflaming the wound will be guarded against.

In all accidents it is important to have the doctor sent for immediately, as they may prove more serious than you suppose.

In a short letter we cannot touch upon many things we would wish, but surely those of us who have been in classes where regular doctors have taught us what to do so as to be able to give "first aid to the injured," are glad of the knowledge obtained, and want to advise other girls to enter similar classes.

There are many small emergencies which can hardly be called accidents. In the country a wasp may sting us, and we should know that spirits of ammonia will relieve the smart ; a slice of an onion or even a piece of damp earth will have the same effect.

In travelling a cinder gets in our eye, occasioning much bother ; get your travelling companion to roll the upper lid over a pencil or knitting-needle, and see if with a handkerchief she cannot find the speck ; or if alone, pull down the upper lid over the under, and try to wink. Lime in the eye can be removed by milk.

A fish-bone gets into your throat, and you commence to choke. Tickle the throat with the finger or a feather to produce vomiting, if you cannot push down or draw out the bone by your finger.

A slight bruise or mashed finger and such things are easily taken care of. Wrap the bruised part in bandages kept wet with cold water, and if the pain is bad put a little arnica or Pond's Extract with the water.

Chilblains can be relieved by bathing the feet in cold water or rubbing with snow. Do not go near the fire, as the heat will aggravate, not relieve.

Sunstrokes need much the same treatment—namely, by the free use of ice-cold water for the head and body.

Vomiting must be brought on if you imagine that any poison has been swallowed ; this can be done by the tickling before spoken of, or by the swallowing of warm, sweetened water.

Little things left to run on often give more trouble than big matters immediately attended to. Thus sprains are frequently more troublesome than a broken limb. If your foot has suddenly received a turn and you are suffering, yet can walk, don't try to do so, but hasten home and attend to it. Put the limb in as *hot* water as you can bear, have this changed until all the inflammation has disappeared ; then keep the foot up and at rest for some time.

A friend of mine has been suffering now from lameness for five months because when he turned his foot he went on to a day's work and used it, until he had to be brought home in an agony of pain, and has had much to bear since.

Girl friends, let us be ready to help in any of the above or other emergencies of daily life, and bravely and well prove ourselves worthy of respect and confidence, no matter where we may be placed.

Cordially yours,

G. H. D.

WORKING AND SAVING.

DEAR GIRLS :

We are all workers—busy bodies ; and I think there is not one of us who could not say, " It seems as if woman's work was never done." Some of us have home cares, and from the making of the fire before six o'clock until nine or ten at night, when the children or family are in bed, we have few idle moments. We find so much to do even in our small rooms or houses. Others of us are due at seven o'clock at factory or shop, and have eight or nine hours of manual work, with only lunch time off. When we get home, if there is no housework there is sewing or planning for clothes, and if we find time for any recreation or fun, we are wondrous busy up to a late hour. Again, there are some of us who use our fingers, and as dressmakers it is sew, sew, sew until we get tired of needles and thread. Still there are among us those who have brain work combined with hand effort, and as teachers, tele-

graph operators, stenographers, clerks, or bearing
still heavier responsibility, we come to night tired
both in body and in mind. Some are ashamed of
being called workingwomen, but why should we
be ? Is it not a grand thing to be a worker, and to
have ability to work ? Nowadays hundreds of girls
are proud of being workers who might stay at home
and be supported by father or mother. They wish
to feel able to care for themselves. No honest work
degrades us, rather uplifts and strengthens us. I
like to feel myself a worker, and to count as true
friends many who labor from early to late in shop
or factory. From the beginning of this world of
ours people have been workers, receiving only
what they or their parents worked for. Some of
those men and women whom you envy and think
of as having a good time always, are much busier
than you ever thought of being, and bear burdens
of responsibility which you can hardly grasp even
in thought. The motto taken by a Prince of Wales
hundreds of years ago, and still borne by the present
prince, translated contains only these two words,
" I serve ;" so, dear girls, if the Prince of Wales
feels the need of such a motto, surely we, too,

should think of ourselves as serving or working.

When we are at home we serve for love, from a
sense of duty, but when we go out from home into
any position we expect to serve for more than these
things—for *money*.

Here, then, are the two points of our letter to-
day—Work, Money ; serving, and the wage received
for said service.

The terms can be applied from the President of
the United States, who serves his country and receives for his work a salary from the country, to a
little cash-girl working for $1.50 per week. Some
of us work hard and find our duties irksome ; some
make light of everything, and by their way of
going about it make all effort easy.

First. Set your mind on the work, whatever it is,
feeling it is necessary and cannot be shirked. Second. When the mind is fixed and it is to be done, try
and take a cheery view of the work. There are
two words which are often used, " Don't worry."
Apply them to the work to be done, and put after
them, " over it." Third. Endeavor by system and
order to simplify the work. Bring your brains to

it and try to lighten it by planning for it, keeping all implements, from pen, pencil, needle, thread, to machinery, in order. Know where your working tools are, and be able to lay your hands on them at any moment.

How often I have seen a girl stop in the midst of a rush of work at home, at the store, or in the work room, and cry out as she hurried around, "Oh, where's my brush?" "Where's the cash-book?" "Where's my scissors?" That quarter of an hour's work is hard, and if the same difficulty continues, at night the girl is tired out and blames the work, when she should blame herself for care-lessness and thoughtlessness. Fourth. Put your heart into your work. This means much the same as the first point, only the addition of love for it and a determination to really do it as well as one can. Heartily, as applied to a hand-shake, you un-derstand; think of the same idea in doing what you have to do to-day, and see if "heartiness" will not help it on. Fifth. Do the work as well as you can, and try and take pride in the doing. Sixth. Make the work yours for the time being, and even if it is done for others, feel it your own, and

show interest in it. Seventh. Quiet, slow work
usually tells better in the long run than that done
with rapid, spasmodic effort, which, while it may
accomplish much in an hour, cannot be continued
for eight hours. The fable of the tortoise and the
hare can be applied here. Eighth. It is hardly necessary to add the thought of faithful, thorough
work. No one will ever succeed or be advanced
who does not do earnest, true work. I have heard
it said that one reason why women cannot compare
with men as " wage-earners" is, that they do not
do faithful, thorough work, for they do not think
of work as a life pursuit, but rather as a necessary
means of tiding over those years before they marry,
and have some man to do the money-earning for them.

Girls, I would not like to think this true, but
rather to feel that we women are so anxious to become skilful, thorough workers that we at all times
are doing our utmost to fit ourselves for that duty
which is ours. Happy women also, for we realize
that we must work, and are doing the best we can
in a cheery, earnest manner.

Because there are so many who have to work and
so many who are not skilled to do anything well,

the amount of money most of us can earn per week
is small.   There are also certain expenses connected
with our work which break into this sum, such as
car fares, taxes, fines, etc., so the dollars we have
on hand pay nights are few and the wants are many.

What are we to do ? We must realize the value of
money.   So few of us really think of what money
is, or, if we do think, of how it can be used.   A
dollar is a hundred pennies, yet a penny means little to us.

Once when discussing this subject with a large
gathering of girls, some one said, " What can one do
with a penny ?" Many replied, " Nothing ;" others,
" Buy a stick of candy with it ;" " Give it to the
children," said another. This suggested farther
inquiry, and some one went to investigate. Several women with small candy-shops or baskets were
visited and questioned. What was the result ?
Why, that these women were supported well by
the pennies which no one knew what to do with.
One queer old character said " that the poorer a
family was the more the children had to spend."
" Why," she continued, " I often and often have
young people come in to buy taffy whose parents'

furniture was lying on the sidewalk, turned out by a landlord because they had not anything to pay their rent." The old proverb says, " Take care of the pennies and the dollars will take care of themselves." Have we learned to care for the one-cent pieces ?

Experience has taught me, as it has other girls, that as long as a five or a two-dollar bill remains in my purse I seem very rich ; but once have the amount broken and silver given back as change, I do not know where it goes to.

Thrift means making the most of one's money, and never spending it unnecessarily. A thrifty girl will make fifty cents go as far as another would a dollar. The same girl can often cut out a dress from twelve yards for which the other would require eighteen, and so on in housekeeping and other matters.

Economy is another word to use here—economy of time, strength, material, and food, as well as money. These matters are so closely allied that we cannot think of saving money without also thinking of saving in other ways, for whatever is saved prevents our getting other things which cost money.

Let me illustrate some little ways of saving : When a bundle comes home, untie and roll up the string, fold the paper, and in a box or bag keep these. Soon we have a bundle to send off, paper and string are needed, and if we have them at hand at least five cents are saved.

Medicines are needed. In another nook we have carefully washed and put away bottles of various sizes from some former sickness. One or two are taken when we go with our prescription, and the druggist allows on them from five to ten cents.

Letters come to us, we tear off the half or quarter sheet, and keep them in our writing folio or box. Suddenly we need a little memorandum-book or slip to write a message on, or we are going to write to a sister or mother ; our saved scraps of paper give us what we now require, and a penny sheet is saved.

In cooking and housekeeping there are endless ways of saving pennies. Ten cents a day *saved* means $36.50 a year, or about what some family's coal and wood bills come to when they buy by the ton and basket.

Here are three rules for shopping which, if followed out, will save you money : Be as careful of small amounts as large. Think twice before buying. Never buy because a thing is cheap.

How many of you keep accounts ? Judging from my girl friends, I should say very few—perhaps not more than one in every ten. You worked hard for $5, and yet would find it difficult to tell me what you did with it—that is, if you had gone out shopping with it in your pocket and came back with only change.

Of course the largest proportion of your money goes into the family purse and is spent by the mother or eldest sister, who is housekeeper, or board is paid by it ; but there are none of us who do not have some pocket money. How do we know where it has gone to at the week's end ? Commence to enumerate : fifty cents for gloves, forty for muslin, a gingham dress for $1.50, and so on ; but there was a dollar more ; what did you do with that ? How was it spent ? You cannot tell, I cannot, and so there was lost a dollar for which you can give no account. It probably went in little trifles which seemed too *small* to be thought of.

Personal accounts for the small sums of money

we have are very easy to keep, and they will be a great help to us in many ways. Buy a penny cash-book with ruled lines. On the left-hand page, at the top, put the word Receipts ; then the month. Now put down any sum you have from your mother or as wages, and set opposite the date of its being received. Add later in the month other amounts, and add all up the first of next month. On the opposite right-hand page put Expenditures, and the month. Put down here what you spend, even a penny for candy or a five-cent car fare. Don't wait for the end of the week, but daily write out the list. After the month is over add this up, put it under the received amount on left page, and deduct from that. Thus : Received, $5 ; expended, $4.68, and you have a balance of thirty-two cents. This is what you saved during the month. It can be carried to the next month, or can be put into a bank as the nucleus of a larger sum.

You will thus be able at a glance to know just how much you have made and how much you have spent for various matters. If the accounts are personal, how much for dress, how much for charity, how much for candy (do be careful that the latter sum is not larger than the former), how much for car fares, and how many cents went in simple pleasure.

If you have household money, accounts are absolutely necessary, so that you can tell how much you spend from month to month.

One girl told me after she had begun to keep accounts how startled she was to find that she had spent in one week fifty cents for candy. Soon her book showed that five cents or no money at all was down for that cause. Another began to realize how quickly two-cent cream cakes amounted up, and came in one day with twenty-five cents for a special matter that the girls were saving for, saying, "Here come twelve cream-cakes which would have all been eaten now, as I commenced to go without only a week."

A bank is an institution we know little about, and yet it is a place we should be familiar with. Few of us think that small sums can go in banks. One dollar or less can be put in at a time, and the feeling that you have a bank-book spurs you on to having more and more figures put in it.

I heard the other day a story of a young colored

girl. She had been at a school where the pupils had a savings-bank arrangement, and for a few years she had saved her odd pennies without much thought. She married, set up housekeeping, and after a time was in great trouble. Her husband was sick, rent was due, all his savings had gone. In despair she went to borrow of her old teacher. When she stated her case the lady said, " But, Mary, you have money." She denied it with almost indignation.

The lady arose, went to a drawer, and handed her a child's bank-book ; it was her own, and to her credit stood about fifteen dollars—enough to cover her debt and to start her family afresh. The girl had forgotten the childish days and the pennies, but there they were awaiting her.

Such emergencies will come to you, too ; will you have anything put by ?

Hoping that we workers may be able to understand how grand a thing it is to be able to work, and trusting that we will also learn to use and keep what we gain, I remain

Your working friend,
G. H. D.

WOMANHOOD—PURITY.

DEAR FRIENDS :

We come to-day to a most earnest subject, with feelings that the matters to be talked over are almost too sacred to speak of, still are of such vital importance to each one of us that we cannot pass them by—I mean those questions that touch upon the special life of women and their beautiful meanings ; also of the true ideas of purity and modesty.

We women are wonderful creations, and we do not half realize the blessed privileges that are ours, and what trusts have been given us. To you may come children ; and you do not want a puny, sickly baby such as you see so often, but rather one healthy and strong ; and to insure this you must take care of your own health. What you are your children will be in great part.

As one means of caring for yourselves, you must most carefully bathe all sacred hidden organs, but in no other way ever touch or think of them.

Oh, dear girl friends, stop and think, are we guilty of thoughts or actions impure or wrong? If so, do hesitate and strive with yourself to overcome. It is hard, very hard, yet we want to have our bodies pure, and in truth fit temples for the Spirit which has been given us.

They are ours in trust only, and we have by and by to render an account. All the secrets of life will then be known. Have we any we will be ashamed of? God help us each to live only for His glory, inside and out. Womanhood should suggest the term modesty. We as girls want to be modest in every respect. We want it in our dress, our actions, our persons. Even when little children modesty should begin. We should be careful in bathing and in performing necessary actions before fathers and brothers. The latter at night should be kept separate from the girls. No sleeping together should be allowed. Screens are most useful, and curtains hung on strings. These are cheap ways of making distinct parts to the same room, and hiding from each other when we are to be in any way exposed.

Wherever we are we are surrounded by temptations.   I have had many a poor girl friend, whom I have met at a time of terrible disgrace and sorrow, who has cried out in her agony, " Oh, warn other girls.   Tell them my story, and prevent them from being where I am.''   Can I do anything but heed ? Here is one of the stories :

A girl, pretty and attractive, one who had been brought up at church and Sunday-school, who yet was fond of fun and attention.   She met a young man, knew nothing about him, but allowed him " to keep company" with her.   Soon he pretended love for her, began to show her attentions.   She liked these and let them go on, thinking he was honorable and true, but instead he was full of wrong intent, and brought to her a life of suffering and shame.

Girls, this story is only too common, and we know of houses full of girls kept for evil.   We are saddened at the thought, and look with scorn at them when we meet them ; rather it should be pity. These girls are young like ourselves, were once pure and innocent, sat perhaps beside some of us at school or church.   Temptation came to them, they yielded, and often by the love which should have brought honor and joy they fell, and sorrow and grief is now their share.

I have talked with these girls. I realize how easy it was for them to fall, and I cannot help coming in their name to you with warnings.

We cannot hold ourselves too valuable. If we are now pure in heart we must shrink from the very beginning of evil, from the light word, the careless jest, the immodest glance.

God has given a conscience that will warn you of the approach of evil. Listen to it! The common excuse, " I thought no harm," is not often a good one, for the voice warned us. But " it was such fun ;" " I was having such a good time," is instead the true excuse.

As was said in one of our other letters, it is not wrong to have men friends, nor wrong to have pleasant times with them. What is wrong is the trying to attract the attention of strangers, the allowing too great intimacies, the joking and " carrying on" which girls think fun, the being out late at night with a man, the going with them to places where you should feel blushes at the sights before you.

It is dangerous as well as wrong to allow a man

to give you money or presents of value, to accept invitations from one you do not know all about, to put yourselves in any way in a man's power.

Engagement is not marriage, and during it you must be on your guard. Think of the difference between a *promise of marriage* and *an actual marriage* itself. There must be no rough freedom, no romping caresses, no behavior that you would be ashamed of if the engagement should be broken.

There are girls who, instead of looking on their honor as their choicest possession, lightly throw it away on the promise of a marriage. When God has joined a man and woman together no one can put them asunder ; but any union before is *sin*.

I want to say something here which will, I think, touch some of us, and that is, that there are other duties and pleasures besides those which come from marriage. So many of us think that " getting married " is the one necessary thing in the world. It is our aim and desire from young girlhood up, and we are so afraid we won't get a husband, we take the first man who pays us attention.

Marriage is a beautiful thing when founded on true respect and love, but, girls, I would rather that we all died " old maids" than that we should be in a hurry, and take a man just " because we want to get married." " Old maid " is not a pleasant term to us, and we shrink from the state which it suggests ; but it is often a very happy thing. The unmarried daughters, sisters, friends, are most necessary and useful in many a home. Happiness and love come to them in caring for nieces, nephews, either real or adopted. A bright, helpful life can be theirs, and as a true, pure woman they can bring cheer and gladness into many a home instead of only one. Their influence over others can be great.

Don't let us make fun of old maids, but rather think, " I may be one myself, and if I am, shall I not make myself valued and loved, even if not by a special few ?"

May I now again, in the name of other poor girls, give you a few distinct warnings. Don't take any liquor or lighter drink with a man. Drugs to stupefy have been used by unscrupulous men, and if taken, you are then in their power.

Look well into any proposed situation, and see how you will be placed. Be careful on the street to attract as little notice as possible, and beware of advances from strangers.   Don't be out alone with a man late in the evening.

Now as to our influence over men.   We have it, dear girls ; there is not one of us who has not more or less influence over some man or boy.   You do recognize your power ; do you use it in trying to make them truer and nobler ?

There has been among some of us a strange feeling, and that is, that men must " sow their wild oats," and that if they sin or do wrong they can be pardoned, while we girls would be turned from all respectable society in disgrace.

It is as right for a man to be pure and good as for a girl, and it injures our purity if we speak lightly of evil in a man friend or to him.   It has been said " that the salvation of man must come through woman."   She must know her power to attract, and use that power in every good way and work.

A man will quickly recognize when we show him we disapprove of him, and that we will not allow liberties taken either with ourselves or with others.

By our strength and purity we can help him. Are we helping our men friends and our brothers to nobler life ?

Many a girl has asked, Is it wrong to dance, to go to the theatre, etc. ? I am not able to answer these questions for you except in a general way, by saying that it is wrong to do anything or to be anywhere that suggests to us foolish, impure thoughts.

Now, at the close of this letter, may I not urge upon each one of you to go to your mother or to some Christian friend and ask questions about any puzzling matter ? Show them this, and ask them to explain points in it you do not understand. If you know me, come freely to me, and let us alone talk over these things.

Be proud that you are a woman, as I am, and try with me to make our womanhood a strong, helpful one, pure, modest, and bright ; one that will reach out and help those who come in contact with us, as Christ our Saviour has reached out and is ready to help any that will come to Him.

Your friend,

G. H. D.

CHARACTERISTICS.

DEAR FRIENDS :

"Characteristics" is defined in the dictionary as that which marks the character ; and " character," as peculiar quality. What are our peculiarities ? There are no two of us alike, and it seems as if it would be interesting for us to talk together on paper, and see if we can find out our own characteristics.

Farther, see if by studying certain other qualities we can be roused to want some we have not now.

A character is a very important thing in one reading of the word, and there are none of us who would not prize a piece of paper given us by a teacher, a friend, an employer, if on it were written words which would make us valued wherever we went, for they would tell of faithful service in school, work, or church, and be a guarantee of the future. I want now to look beyond such a meaning to the word, and just take up one after the other attributes which tend to form us or our character.

A little girl once contracted the habit of calling herself " Dear me," and as she went around always said, " Dear me wants so and so," or, " Won't you give that to Dear me ?" The words we are all familiar with, " Oh, dear me !" is a common expression. Do you think it symbolizes one of your attributes, thinking first of " me," making it *dear* to yourself ? It is called selfishness, and is recognized when a girl's first thought is for herself. It was " Dear me" when we were little and saw one apple or piece of cake on the plate, and took it first ; " Dear me" later, when we took the best seat, or insisted upon an extra dress, which cost our mother so much effort to make ; " Dear me" when we now indulge in cross words, when we enjoy our own sulks, and make others suffer ; " Dear me" when our one thought of money is, What will it get for *me ?* or when our work, sewing, effort is all for   lf.

Daughters who let their mothers slave and labor for them with no thought of their weariness have the *dear me* fever badly ; also the sister who, absorbed in her novel, lets the baby cry or brother get angry because she is not ready to forget the book in their wants.

Whole families suffer from one member whose first thought is *dear me ;* also schools and cities, and even our country, for this attribute is at the root of many of the evils of our present government.

Against it we find the element of self-forgetfulness and generosity ; the brightness and joy which come when the first question and thought is, What can I do for some one else ? The girl who is always ready for interests outside of herself, whose happiness comes from following the old rule, " Not to think of self first"—such persons we have met, and how we admire and love them !

But there is a thinking of self which we must not forget—viz., self-respect. Self is of great importance, as we found in discussing dress and health. We must respect ourselves and make others respect us. A girl with hair falling down, dirty collar on, ragged dress, and slovenly look cannot respect herself, and surely no one else will. Again, the girl who allows a young man to take liberties with her, who tries to attract attention on the street, who talks loudly and coarsely, who allows people to take her to places where she sees sights a modest girl ought not to look at, or who will read in a paper things that never ought to be put into print, much less read—can that one admire herself, can she keep her own respect ?

But, dear girls, let me add that your own self-respect or esteem must not be such that you are tempted to be proud of yourself and your goodness, and so look with scorn upon those poor girls who have not had your advantages, and who in consequence have lost their own respect, and have fallen from force of heavy temptation ; rather should you by loving pity look upon such a one and, if possible, give her helping hands.

I have just heard the expression, " She is so lovable," and instantly a picture came to me of a gentle, loving girl who is not pretty, but rather is always neat, trim, and attractive ; who is full of thoughtfulness, and is so bright and sweet that every one loves her. She is a girl who attracts little children, who looks out for old people, and who tries truly to forget self in thinking of other people. This girl has never any money to give, for she lives in a poor tenement-house room ; but where she goes the sunshine seems to follow, and she seems to be sunshine itself. Did you ever meet this girl? How about yourself? Is this attribute, lovable, applicable to you and me?

There are still other characteristics to consider, among them perfect truthfulness and honesty. They seem to belong together. Truthful and honest through and through, outside and inside, are attributes we would all be proud of possessing.

We know well when our milk is not honest, when our sugar does not taste as sweet as it should, and shows that it is not truthful, honest sugar. We hear of thieves, of those who take other people's things, and we feel ourselves not like these things or persons; but, girls, I wonder if we are truthful always in what we say of other people; if we exaggerate their faults and failings; if in ourselves we show out truth. Are we honest in our dealings— not in big things, I mean, but in all little transactions? That grocer probably considers himself honest, and yet he it was who put the pint of water in our quart of dishonest milk, and the mixture with the real sugar that took from its strength. It seemed a little thing to him, and yet to us it was dishonest.

In our home life, our friendships, in our work, are we honest? May I confess here that it is a hard thing to me to be so in all my words and actions, and yet I do strive, and know that by trusting in a Higher Strength I can succeed.

Just stop for a moment before going to bed some night and see how it has been with you. Especially ask yourself if you have been true and honest, if during the day you have been having a good, old-fashioned gossip. We all enjoy what is called a gossipy talk, but do be careful.

Did you ever hear such expressions as these—" I didn't think," " I forgot," or, " I was in such a hurry I didn't remember" ? I have often heard these words. They bear upon an idea which seems deep rooted in even children's minds. I wonder if it is a very good excuse to make when we say " I didn't think ;" should we not have thought ? Would we have taken cold if we had thought and brought our rubbers or a heavy jacket, when we might have known it would probably rain or suddenly become cold ? Would that cup have broken if we had thought and put it farther on the table ? Would our mother's feet be so tired if the daughter's head had remembered that she might be tired? Would it not be easier to make up the fire in the morning if some one had thought the night before to lay out the kindling and paper?

When we come in from down-town, would it be much of an excuse to say, " Oh, I forgot," when our sister asked if we had remembered to buy her ribbon or spool of cotton?

Much discomfort and even sorrow would be saved the world if we could *remember* and have no excuses to make, such as " I didn't think."

Carelessness goes on the same page of our catalogue of attributes. It is apt to follow upon " I forgot," and then there comes an expression " I don't care." Don't care! Why, you should care. Careful, thoughtful! Planning or thinking ahead, making ready, being ready! Careful about little things, like the order of a bureau-drawer, or the setting of the family breakfast-table, as well as careful in big matters. Dresses, shoes, bonnets, hats, *with care* last twice as long as without. Brains have to be brought into play here.

A visitor once asked a celebrated painter with what he had painted the picture before them.

" With brains, sir," was the answer. We do not
paint scenes, but we *live* them, and I wish we could
all bring the brains into every day, and think more
before acting.

We would have attained that other quality then,
of always being trustworthy, or worthy of trust.

King Solomon, in his picture of a good wife of
olden time, said, " Her husband could always safely
trust in her." Let us aim to become such wives.

Did you ever think who does the " odd jobs" in
the world ? One often says, " Oh, that is not my
work ; I won't do it." If every one said this there
would be many an odd job no one would do, and
much would be thus left undone.

There are happily some people who are the pleasant, obliging people, who run here and there and do
this and that which they see wants doing, without
ever stopping to ask, " Is it my business ?" These
people do not work for thanks, and they seldom
get thanks ; but there is an eye watching them, and
the Christ who Himself while here on the earth did
all the little kindly deeds and all the hard work that
there was to be done is watching. He knows and
loves the doer.

Let us this next week see if there are not some odd jobs we can do. There is an old saying reading thus: "Something disagreeable has to be done, somebody must do it; find a good reason why you are not the somebody." I therefore expect this week that you girls will be the "somebodies" to do the disagreeable things you will surely meet, for you will not be able to give yourselves a good reason why you should not do them.

Here we have been discussing some ten or more characteristics. Count them up on your fingers and name them; then shut down all those fingers whose names are attributes you have not got. How many have you left? Again, lift up those you would like to have. How many are these? Why not have them? What hinders you from being unselfish, thoughtful, self-respecting, lovable, truthful, honest, careful, trustworthy, obliging, generous?

"A great deal," you say. Yes, I know, dear girl friends, for I know from my own experience. All I can say is, let us try, and "if we don't succeed, then try, try again." We need help, and it will be ours.

Nearly nineteen hundred years ago there lived

here a man who in Himself was combined these and many other lovable qualities. He was the embodiment of all that our highest thoughts could conceive of love and perfectness. His presence is still here, for He said, " Lo, I am with you always," and again said, " Ask and ye shall receive."

Let us, then, pray and ask that man Christ, our divine Saviour, for strength to gain those characteristics which will make us more earnest, happy girls, and which will be to us a mine of strength and wealth when we are women.

These attributes will fit us to be true wives and mothers, helpful sisters, friends, and from us will go out brightness and cheer to those many we come into contact with. We will be ourselves examples to them, and let our example be such as we would have them follow.

With best wishes for each of you, I am

Truly your friend,

G. H. D.

FOUR INTERESTING QUESTIONS.

DEAR FRIENDS :

Among the influences which affect our lives there are few greater than the answers to the following questions : Who are our friends ? How do we talk with them ? What kind of letters do we write and receive ? What books most interest us ?

Four points only, and yet if I could feel that you would answer them frankly, I would be sure that I know you and your real inner life.

I have heard some one say, " A girl is known by the company she keeps," and I cannot help but feel that it is true.

A friend ! This word means much. It suggests one who is in thorough sympathy with you, one whom you like to be with, and with whom you can talk and tell out your thoughts. One must also trust a true friend, and feel that she is faithful and devoted to you as you are to her. Much of the happiness and purity of our lives depends on our choosing wise companions and friends. Most of us trust in this matter to chance, and pick up any one whom we casually meet and call them friends. I would rather say acquaintances.

There is a great difference in these two words. It is right to be courteous and considerate to every one with whom we come in contact, but to choose them as real friends is another matter.

Again, it is not always those who live the nearest to us nor those who are relatives whom we feel are our friends.

We need companionship and society, but be careful as to the influence which comes from it. It must be helpful or the reverse.

How is it with you ? After spending an after-noon or evening with your friends, how do you feel ? You have had a good time, yes ; but has it been a time satisfying to you ?

It is hard to answer when some one questions, " How can I choose my friends ?" Discrimination comes in here, and sensibility. Some people seem to be had for the asking, and all they have to give you they give right away, and give to everybody the same. The girl who kisses you with as keen

enjoyment as if she had known you for years, the
one who on a day's acquaintance tells you the history of her love experiences, or private family matters, possibly is sincere, but her manner is against
her, and you would not feel as if you could trust her,
for she is too much like a sieve, and should be told
nothing except what you want known to all the
world.

There are others who at first hold aloof and seem
cold, but soon you begin to know them better, they
thaw out, let you gradually into their lives, and by
their interest in you draw out from you your best
thoughts and ways. They seem full of sympathy,
and become the most delightful of companions, for
you feel you can rest on them, and they will understand you. These friends are rarely selfish, and
do not think that your entire life must be absorbed
in them, and that you must not love any one but
themselves. "A sweet reasonableness must lie at
the root of all true friendship." We must expect
our friends to make allowances for us, and we in
our turn must be ready to make allowances for them.

Falseness is fatal to friendship, as also acts of un-
kindness. The idea of service comes here. Serve

one another. Try and please in little ways as well as big, and use influence for good.

Do our friends flatter and caress us ? If so, are they true ? We consult each other in our troubles and perplexities, and should receive helpful advice, such as is wise and calm. Friends should by their faith as well as advice strengthen and cheer.

If you have a true friend, don't let a misunderstanding or bit of gossip turn you against her. Don't believe stories told you until you can go to that friend and have a frank talk with her. Explanations will probably clear away much that has been hard to understand. A true friend you cannot afford to lose.

Acquaintances you must not confound with the word friends, as we have said, and each must be distinct in your mind. The acquaintance will probably leave you alone in time of sorrow or disgrace ; the friend will stick all the closer. In such times friendships are fostered and acquaintanceships broken up. Among those you go with, which are friends, which acquaintances ?

There are people who call themselves friends, and all they do is to be finding fault, saying, " It's all for your good." Such are useful sometimes in showing us our faults, and perhaps they are truer friends to us than some who may flatter us to our faces and speak evil of us behind our backs.

Just two words more to remember—constant! loyal! With these our friendships will be to us blessings and joys, and sources of true strength.

Old Dr. Samuel Johnson was once asked, "Have you had a pleasant evening?" "Oh, yes," was the answer, "for, sir, we had a good talk." Since then and before it has been talk, talk, talk. It is incessant; wherever we are, people are talking. We ourselves talk a large percentage of our lives.

"The tongue is a little member, but it boasteth of great things." This is wonderfully true. We show ourselves in our talk.

There is family talk, society talk, business talk, loving talk, angry and cross talk, learned talk, careless talk, good and bad talk. Language shows the mind and the condition of the heart. Words roll out so easily that no thought is given them; they come wherever we are and in whatever circumstances.

Perhaps you once had a cold and could not

speak. Do you remember how you wanted to, and how hard it was to keep quiet ? Then you realized the value of words, and how good it is to be able to talk. I sometimes wish that more people had constant colds, so that their talk need not come to me, it is so trying and hard to bear.

Just stop and think about your tongue, girls ; what does it do for you ? What kind of talk is yours ? Is it cheery, good, bright ? Free from coarse, vulgar expressions, free from complaints and crossness ? Is it helpful or the reverse to the friends and acquaintances, for by means of talk we communicate with these.

Conversation can be made one of the best means for study and improvement. None of us who for years have enjoyed the Tuesday evenings can help testifying to the value of practical talks. Do you remember how often one of you have come to me and said, " Oh, we need a good, old-fashioned talk ; won't you have it with us ?" We sit right down and take up first one point, then another, until some difficulties have vanished, and we feel strengthened to go out and meet the perplexities of life. Such conversations I have had also with many an individual friend, gentleman and lady. They have helped me, and I have helped them just by our mutual words.

If you want to influence a friend, there is no greater way than by words, either written or spoken—that is, if your actions show your words true. We do not want to be hypocrites in our talk, saying one thing and thinking and doing another. Rather we want language to express the truest, strongest part of ourselves, and be our means of helping others and ourselves.

Here are a few points to avoid in talking : Exaggeration ; saying behind a person's back disagreeable things which you would not say to her ; unkind speeches, which leave sore spots behind ; foolish expressions ; slangy words, which mean so little ; any allusion to coarse, vulgar matters ; repeating stories about any one which do not sound well of them.

The time when we should specially be on our guard is in society. Here we often get excited and forget ourselves, and talk on and on in a wild sort of way, which we are very sorry for afterward. I think there is not one of us who has not some time felt ashamed of a conversation in which we took part at some party or picnic.

Men seem also to excite girls, and they will so far forget themselves with them that their language means much more than it should. Let a guard be kept on our tongues, dear friends. There is not one of us who does not need to do this.

The tongue should be a good, faithful servant, who does not need reproof, rather praise for always being truthful, kind, and tactful. This last word implies so much. Tact is knowing just when to speak or act and when to be quiet.

Letter-writing means simply written talk. Years ago it was an expensive luxury, enjoyed rarely, and by only a few. Now with our cheap paper and postage, letter-writing has so multiplied that a small army of men are kept busy with the postal service, and millions of dollars are yearly spent on *letters.*

The mail is always interesting, and whenever we hear the postman's whistle or walk to the post-office, the thought is, " Oh, I wonder if I have a letter !" Yes, there it is, bringing good or bad news, with nice matter or disagreeable.

As letters are only written talk, we can apply to

them all that has been said. But spoken words may be forgotten, they pass away. Written words do not. They are fixed in pen and ink, and their effects will often linger long after any talk would have been forgotten. So we must have special care in writing talk.

I am sure none of us will agree with the old lady who said all love-letters are rubbish ; perhaps, as she never married, she had not received one herself ; but in writing or receiving such letters we must not forget caution. It is a dangerous habit to commence correspondence with men. Often such an imprudence will lead to a sad ending. A letter written on an impulse or by an excited imagination may become, in the hands of an unprincipled man, a terrible instrument of torture. Hundreds of women would give anything to be able to efface the written words held in another's possession.

Let us repeat in the language of some one else : " I am always doubly careful what I write ; for what I say may be forgotten, but what I put down in black and white is always there to bear witness against me if I make a mistake."

We do not know what becomes of our letters ;

whether they are torn up or put into the fire and meet no eyes but those that they were meant for, or whether they are put away, and come out long years after for good or evil, when we have forgotten all about them. Letters are wonderful helps or hindrances to friendships. I have talked on paper with many a friend whom I have not seen for years. If we can only feel that friendship and these methods of communication, either spoken or written, are talents given us to use ; also that our Heavenly Friend, who Himself has left us conversations and written letters, is interested in the use we give these talents, we will surely endeavor to use them for His glory and for our own and others' good.

Our fourth question is untouched, and yet it is as important as the rest. Books are most satisfactory friends. They entertain and help us as little else does.

When, years ago, letters were rare, books too were few. They were valuable, and only owned by a certain class of people. Now we have too many books. Too much to read. We can enjoy or appreciate none as we should.

One day last summer a girl only fourteen told me

that since school closed she had read sixty story-books. I questioned her about them, and she could tell me nothing of what she had *read*, and hardly could tell the titles of the books. What good did they do her?

Books are meant to be read and remembered. As means of education they are valuable. In lonely times they are companions. They should be helps and not hindrances to our life.

A taste for books and good reading can be culti-vated. As a means of influence in our lives, books rank very high. So good books, as helpful friends, will make us stronger and better, while silly news-papers and books must bear fruit, and make us re-semble the paper or book. Some books make us unsettled, and we feel that our life is very hard and uncomfortable, and we wish that some prince would come along and take us from its drudgery, as the rich man did in our novel. We wish after reading it that we might be some one else and have a good time. We are so dissatisfied with ourselves.

Such books cannot help us, and they had better be unread. Many stories that come out in the weekly papers are equally bad, if not worse. They are very interesting and we love to read them, but they are harmful to us. Indeed, I often wish there were no newspapers, for they seem so unsatisfactory. They are full of tragedies, horrors, and unfortunate matters which only harm us in hearing of them.

Now that there are so many free and circulating libraries, none of us should say we can get nothing worth reading. We can, indeed, find good books ; but the trouble is, so few care to read them.

Here are some of the matters which are taken up in a catalogue of books : Biography, which tells of real lives that have been lived, and which should act as inspiration, showing us what some one did and was. History, which records struggles and achievements of mankind in the past, and is full of instructive facts. Travel, which treats of surroundings far off, and transports us in fancy to far-distant scenes, showing us the vastness and wonder of the world. Poetry, delightful to those who enjoy it, as it rouses the imagination and helps to uplift thoughts.

Then there is light science, botany, essays, and many other subjects.

But you say the most interesting point has not

been touched. No; and it seems hardly necessary
to speak of novels or stories—those books which
treat of " lots of love," as you girls say when you
come to me for a book.

A good story is not bad reading, and will often
help us ; but the foolish ones, full of false sentiment,
the books with plots of wickedness and sin, those
which touch upon evil questions—these are to be
avoided.

Do make companions of books, and select wise
friends who will interest and strengthen.

Your true friend,
G. H. D.

GREATEST MATTERS OF ALL.

Dear Girl Friends :

How many interesting matters we have been discussing together! It seems as if such talks must do us good, for they affect us so very closely. You and I are together in all these things, and together we have been learning practical home truths.

We have, however, left some questions untouched, and these are among the highest.

In almost every home circle there are young lives— the children of the house, our own brothers or sisters, our nieces and nephews, or our friends' little ones. These influence us, and most surely we influence them either for good or bad.

It almost seems hard that a man's or woman's life is based largely upon the early training and surroundings. Indeed, the mother's and father's life before their birth has its influence, for as we can say, "Baby's eyes are just like his father's," or

" How like Mary is to her mother !" " Did you
ever see such a resemblance ?" so we truly see how
like, in temperament and personal characteristics,
the child is to the parents.

It is a solemn thought that our faults may be re-
peated in other lives, but so means the saying,
" Oh, Tom has a temper like his father," or, " She
is just as sweet and loving as her mother was."
Happily parents are not always reduplicated, but it
is a probable thing, and needs attention.   Children
are the beginnings of the men and women who, after
twenty or more years, are to fill the places we now
occupy.   They can be made true, noble representa-
tives, or the reverse.   Shall we not strive to put our
influence on the right side ?

I am sorry for the children, they are so rarely
understood or appreciated.

They live in the present, and give little thought
to the past or future.   To-day, this week, or now
is their horizon, and in this time are crowded sorrows and joys, disappointments and happy surprises, perplexities and sore hurts, as real and hard
to bear to them as our life experiences are to us.
The broken doll for the moment is a real grief ; the

sense of being misunderstood and being treated with injustice is most vital to them ; and they too are often bidden to bury their sorrows and hurts in bleeding hearts, as we older ones are told to hide our sorrows.

Children have keen sensibilities, and these are not appreciated. A grumbling, fault-finding parent or care-taker over children will harm the child, for the thought will be, " What's the good of trying to do right, I never can please mother or sister !" Therefore, please don't nag a young one.

Then the careless person, who does not care to take the trouble to do either morally or physically for the child—what will be the result in future years ? The one who thinks only of the clothes, and neglects the health and spiritual development ; the mother who is irregular in her discipline and care, one week all attention, the next just the reverse—how will it be with her son and daughter ? The child cannot have such training as will fit it for life's work.

Their dress, their food, their education are most important, and some time perhaps you and I can take these points up in special letters. At this time we can only hint at them, and leave you with these few ideas.

Never tell a child an untruth, either small or large ; never threaten what you know cannot be carried out. Be decided and yet kind ; loving, patient, cheerful, never nagging. Praise as well as blame, remembering further that you are the person that represents life to them, and as you are, so will they be. A great responsibility, is it not ?

All through these pages we have referred to happy, bright people, and often we wonder why some people look always happy and smiling, while others, who are no worse off, look as miserable as possible. Why should one person be happier than another, when there is nothing to make them so ? Does not the one have what the other has not ? Yes, dear friends, she has, and it is well to know what brings true happiness and strength to make strong, joyous lives.

Health is one cause, and so it is well to gain this as far as possible. Another is the training of ourselves to look out for the bright side of things instead of the dark side.

In walking on a cold day, supposing you took that

side which was in shadow, and said to yourself as you kept your head turned to the shade, " I am so cold, it is so dreary to-day ;" would not any one passing by on the other sunny side say, if he heard you, " Of course you are cold and gloomy, because you won't look this side ; if only you will cross over you will be in sunshine."

Well, life is like that street, and you may choose upon which side you will walk.

Make the best of things when you can't escape them. Try to laugh, not cry over accidents and disappointments. Have brave courage. Do not sink under trials, but rise above them.

" But trials are so hard to bear ; no one ever had such hardship," you say. This is indeed apparently true to many of us. As one with you, I, too, have had my trials and hardships, and it is only by exercising will power that I have been able to come to you at times with smiles. Not by trusting in my own will ; this is weak and failing ; but there is a strength greater than mine. This we must look up to.

There is a motto taken by many of us, and not by our organizations alone, but also by thousands of others—" Look up, not down ; look forward, not back ; look outward, not inward, and lend a hand."

Above there is the sky, with its wonderful sun, moon, and stars, showing by their brightness and stability a Power which must be behind them.

Oh, what a Power that is ! The Jehovah, the Creator, and yet by His own message to us the Heavenly Father, the Elder Brother, the Saviour Friend ; truly " His name shall be called Wonderful, Counsellor, the Mighty God, the Everlasting Father, the Prince of Peace."

He is above, yet near. His presence is guiding and watching over this earth here, and not the world as a whole, but as composed of individuals.

He said, " I know even the sparrows of the field, and not one can fall without My knowledge."

We, His children, He knows through and through. Look up, then, to His strength, and gain from Him help and power.

He is not so far off that you cannot approach Him. He has given us the privilege of always coming to Him. Prayer means talking with Him. He hears and answers.

" Look forward, not back." Keep the future,

with courageous look, before you. Forget the trials
and hardships of the past, and go forward. This is
but the school-house time, and there is a glorious
future for those who look upward and have trust.

But in looking forward, don't manufacture hardships in the future.

> ' Build a firm fence of trust
>   Around to-day ;
> Look not through the sheltering bars
>   Upon to-morrow.
> God will help you bear what comes,
>   Be it joy or sorrow."

Trials are always harder to bear in imagination
than in reality. To-day meet what comes, in
strength from above, and for the to-morrows don't
worry, but feel that they, too, can be happily borne
with the same trust. Above all, forget the gloom
and darkness of the past, and let the future make
up in brightness for the trials then.

By speaking of brightness I do not mean that
trials may not again come. They probably will ;
but we must know how to so meet them that the
sunshine will ever come with them, and we will
feel that for some wise reason they are for our good.

"Look outward, not inward." Inward glances show us much that is hard and discouraging, but looking out from ourselves, we will see how much we have to be thankful for, for around and outside will be seen so many more forlorn and unhappy than ourselves.

"Lend a hand," or helping other people. How bright this will make our lives! Helping them not by money, but by loving words, smiles, hearty greetings, a flower, a bit of fruit, a letter of sympathy, a giving up of an afternoon or evening of personal amusement to read to a sick friend or to do some sewing for a tired mother; the being kind to children, courteous to the aged, in a thousand and one ways forgetting all about such a person as self, and seeing how much thought for others can be cultivated.

The following are rules of contentment given to young people by an English Friend many years ago:

"1. Allow thyself to complain of nothing, not even of the weather.

"2. Never picture thyself to thyself under any circumstances in which thou art not.

"3. Never compare thine own lot with that of another.

"4. Never allow thyself to dwell on the wish that this or that had been or were otherwise than it was or is.

"5. Never worry over the morrow. Remember that it is God's, not thine. The heaviest part of sorrow is to look forward to it. 'The Lord will provide.'"

Add to these the word love. Love! The word is sacred to me; it tells of the great sacrifice offered once for the world, for us; it tells of that which is freely offered us still, and in return the love is wanted back again.

It is, "Love the Lord thy God with all your heart, soul and mind, and your neighbor as yourself."

Oh, that this spirit might animate each one of us! And with the heartiest of cordial greetings to you all, my dear, busy girl friends, I remain

Faithfully yours,

G. H. D.

THOUGHTS OF
BUSY GIRLS

Cooking for the sick is an art in itself, and one
which I hope you will all know something about;
for a patient's food is often more important than
his medicines.

Don't ever ask a sick person what she wants to
eat. Let the food be unexpected, and served in an
attractive way. Try and keep all idea of eating out
of sight and mind except when the nourishment or
meal must be given. Bring a little in at a time,
and it will probably be found that the food must
be given frequently. Surprises are often most
pleasing, and they especially are enjoyed by a sick
person when they come in the shape of some unexpected dainty or dish. A flower laid on the tray
will interest and make her forget how disagreeable
it is to eat, or some new style of cup or plate will
attract attention and serve the same purpose. Try
above all to bring nothing greasy to a patient, nor
have on the tray any spotted napkin or cloth.

When you were once sick, do you remember how
dreadful it was to hear a door creak, to have a person come into the room with noisy boots on? Do
you not also remember how trying it was to have
the doctor go out on the landing, and then have

THOUGHTS

OF

BUSY GIRLS

*Written by a group of girls who have little
time for study, and yet who find
much time for thinking*

EDITED BY

GRACE H. DODGE

———

NEW YORK

CASSELL PUBLISHING COMPANY

104 & 106 FOURTH AVENUE

THE MERSHON COMPANY PRESS,
RAHWAY, N. J.

TO

THE MANY GIRLS WHO ARE COLABORERS IN

FACTORY, SHOP, OFFICE, HOME,

THESE PAGES ARE

Dedicated

BY THE GIRLS WHO HAVE GIVEN TIME FOR

THOUGHT AND STUDY, AND WHO HOPE

THAT BEFORE LONG ALL GIRLS MAY

LEARN TO VALUE AND LOVE

" PRACTICAL TALKS " AS

MUCH AS THEY DO.

In case of visiting a person with a contagious disease, care must be taken not to go into the room without removing outer clothing, or, if possible, wearing a dress which can be washed. On leaving it one should bathe carefully and remove the clothing soon, especially before going among children. As nurses and visitors too much care cannot be exercised to prevent any spread of the contagion. Doing otherwise may mean innocent murder.

Accidents are constantly occurring. Emergencies come to us, and we must act in them. Strangely, the very first mode of acting must be the keeping cool, quiet, and collected ; ready to help, but if there is nothing that can be done except by the one or two, keeping out of the way of these.

In all accidents the poor person who has met with it must first be given plenty of air, and, secondly, he or she must be kept as quiet and free from excitement as possible. Thirdly, clothing must be loosened.

Think back and see how you all acted the last time there was an accident in the shop, and see which girl you wish to copy. We want to be true women, who are not made foolishly curious, neither

CONTENTS.

INTRODUCTION.

OVER ten years ago a large group of girls, coming from different branches of industrial work, or-, ganized a series of Practical Talks upon matters closely affecting the lives of women. After a while these evenings resulted in the formation of the first working girls' club of New York. Amid the many ramifications and interests, there is no one thing which holds attention, and which has so steadily increased in value, as the Practical Talk night. At first only the leader presented the subject, the rest contenting themselves with discussing the views brought out by her; then on cer-

tain evenings those present gave
their opinions in short, condensed
sentences. Some two years ago
the plan was adopted of having
different members assigned to a
subject, and that these should
open the evening by papers or
speech, the rest preparing themselves to criticise. These evenings have been greatly enjoyed,
and the suggestion arose, Would
not other girls like to share in
part the good times? It has
seemed wise, therefore, to the
members of the Practical Talks
of the Thirty-eighth Street Working Girls' Society to give some of
their ideas to the many who have
not realized that a girl who *must*
work can also *think*. A book was
prepared by the leader and issued
in the form of twelve letters to
girls. This was so kindly received
and started so much interest, that
the demand arose for another
book, or a sequel to " A Bundle of
Letters to Busy Girls." Since it
was issued, the members have so
grown in confidence that their

own words as well as thoughts are now given. The chapters will, therefore, be found to contain several short parts, and in certain instances, after the longer papers, some short sentences giving in a nutshell the argument of the evening. There will be found crudeness of diction, certain repetition, and probably errors of grammar, etc. No excuses are offered, except the general one of no time for educational advantages, as with most of the writers the necessity of earning daily bread came in very early girlhood. Those who have written come to the Club from silk and carpet mills, twine, vest, and tobacco factories, from sewing rooms, flower, and feather work. Others are behind the counters of New York's great stores; certain of them are clerks, stenographers, others tailoresses, while two or three come fresh from the schoolroom. Over fifty writers are represented, some of these in only single sentences. A portion come from very young workers, and these are marked "Juniors." The chapter upon Club Life has been added, hoping that from it others may gain an inspiration, and a desire for the practical working out of the three words, co-operation, self-government, and self-support. These compound words have meant much to those whose ideas are here given, and the "Thoughts of Busy Girls" is simply one of the results of their application.

G. H. D.

CHAPTER I.

WHAT CONSTITUTES AN IDEAL WOMANHOOD, AND HOW TO ATTAIN TO IT.

AN ideal woman is truly womanly in all things; self-sacrificing, gentle, tender, and truthful. She is brave and decided in what she knows is right, yet yielding in matters of little importance. She never speaks evil of others, but tells them their faults in a kind way, yet always tries to find virtues, and to see the best point in everybody. She is helpful to others, generous, conscientious, self-reliant, amiable. In her work she practices the Golden Rule of doing to others as she would be done by. I know of one who possesses all these

qualities; she is a friend to everyone whom she knows. If each
one of us could but try to cultivate such a lovely disposition, we
should perhaps make those around
us more thoughtful of their actions to others. Let us begin by
doing as we would be done by.

F. M.

The ideal woman is more than
a fairy or a goddess; she will be
sure to have as many different
features or countenances as she
has different pens to describe her.
Some will take Susan B. Anthony
for their ideal, and some will be
satisfied with Patience on a monument, or Patience even without
the hope of a monument. The
papers of the day tell us of a famous Count's daughter—Tolstoi's
—who works like a peasant girl
in the field; and she, of course,
believes that is an ideal womanhood. But I think we women
had better leave the fields to the
men, and not deprive them of
Adam's first duty. Women in

Canada have worked in the fields, and have considered themselves paid when they had fifteen cents per day. I do not think the ideal woman will be found in the fields of Canada. I believe that one poet found his ideal woman—Maud Müller—at work in the field, barefooted. Her tough feet do not belong to my ideal woman. I think the engravers are with me, for they always see that Maud Müller is well shod.

One of the loveliest women I have ever known has passed away in her early, lovely womanhood. To describe her is beyond the power of my pen, but I can tell some of her pleasing qualities. She was never angry; she was always cheerful; she was never envious or fault-finding; she was always smiling and encouraging. She was never idle, wasteful, or selfish; she was always trying to help all. Sunshine might have been truthfully her name. It was as much her nature to be good as it is the nature of a rose to be fragrant.

Never in all her life did she say
one word purposely to wound the
feelings of another. One would
never tire of listening to her
pleasant words, or looking into her
bright and smiling face ; she had
many duties as daughter, sister,
wife, mother, and friend, and she
neglected none of them. She was
also a friend to all in need, and a
King's Daughter, if our Christ is
indeed King. Is she not worthy
to be an ideal woman ?

R. N. H.

In the first place, my ideal woman must be modest and womanly,
but not prim. Kind, sympathetic,
and thoughtful for others ; religious and broad in her views, not
too strict or narrow-minded.
Ambitious and independent
enough to have an aim in life, and
work toward the development of
that aim. She must be energetic
and busy all the time, doing her
duty, however small and insignificant, faithfully and well. By setting our standard high, the effort to

reach it will ennoble us even if we fail, I am sure. S. H.

What is my idea of an ideal woman? It seems something strange to ask me the question, a young girl that has hardly attained womanhood. Yet I suppose it means what I would like to be myself, and would like to see in others. If you had asked my idea of the kind of young man I would like best, that would be something that I have thought more of. But to ask me what I think a woman ought to be, makes me think of something I have not studied very much. For when I reckon myself up, to start with, I find I could not get along with another like me at all. I see so many that I would wish to be like; well, not exactly in all their ways; but let 'me take three or four that I know, and let me dissect the part which I like best from each, and put them together; then I think I could produce my ideal woman. But such things being impossible, and I be-

ing so far behind those I would take
a slice from, I will try to picture in
my mind the woman I would like
to be. But I'm afraid, I being so
young and inexperienced, it will
seem very silly to those with older
heads, and I can only carry my
imagination to what I like to see
in a girl in the same walk of life as
myself. That is, one that works
for a living, and about my own
age. My ideal is one with a very
cheerful and lively disposition,
that naturally wants to say something to make you feel good, and
even a little bit naughty. She
must be religious, but I don't like
a perfect saint; I don't care for a
girl that is giddy, that says foolish
things, and is continually laughing
and saying what she thinks are
smart things. I like one that you
can see that she feels what she
says, and is full of sympathy as
well as being cheerful. In my
opinion, a woman that has little
sympathy was intended for a bad
man. Education and wealth
help a little to make my ideal

woman, but she may be found
without either in the working girl
that takes pleasure in learning
all the household duties that a
true woman ought to know, and
leaving alone that work which be-
longs to men, so that when she
gets a home of her own, which she
will be very careful in choosing—
as there are so many bad ones—
she will be a comfort. I am going beyond my depth now, for
mamma says my ideal will need
all the sympathy and patience she
has got, if she has a large family
like ours.   L. D., a Junior.

*Summary of the qualifications
of an ideal woman.*

Purity, honesty, faithfulness,
charity, cheerfulness, consist-
ency, self-forgetfulness, sympathy, thoughtfulness, punctuality,
and possessed of good temper,
patience, principle, strength, tact,
courage, perseverance, neatness,
and common sense.

Thoughts upon a useful life.

To take care of one's health is

the first thing, so that one will have strength to be useful. Try to think of things which are useful and then put them into action.

Learning to do things well that seem commonplace. Learning also that little things count; therefore they are not to be carelessly laid aside or overlooked.

Making use of one's odd moments that are liable to be wasted if we do not watch ourselves closely, thereby wasting many chances that might be used.

To do as much good as possible to those we come in contact with, and try to set a good example to those younger than ourselves.

Not only doing for ourselves, but trying to help others who are not as fortunate as ourselves.

Being as unselfish as possible, and keeping busy for other people.

A life that brings sunshine into the small details of the home, and that forgets self in the welfare of others.

CHAPTER II.

PURITY AND MODESTY: TWO WORDS OF VALUE.

Purity.

FREEDOM from moral defilement is purity. Sins against purity are not only sins against God, but insults to our own nature. We are surrounded by so much that is corrupting that we need all the helps possible to promote our own purity and that of those around us. Women should unite and work for the moral uplifting of their sex, as the men have done in the great movement known as the White Cross Army.

These are some of the dangers threatening our purity: Sensa-

tional articles in newspapers;
novels of a low order; plays that
pander to the sensual passions;
and a lax condition of society
that permits undue familiarity
between the sexes. What can
one do in the struggle for purity
and righteousness?

We must use every means to
fulfill the command, " Keep thyself pure." Remember, we need
a higher power than our own to
overcome evil. Then we must
recognize that we each one of us
in a certain sense are our sister's
keeper. If good, pure women
will not help their fellow-sisters,
who will?   H. J.

Purity in womanhood is the
mark of all true womanhood,
without which it is only a name.
It is God's most precious gift to
woman, and should be guarded
with life, for what is a woman's
life without it? It is a whiteness
of mind and heart that everyone
must have and defend by every
means in her power.

Impure thoughts often bring words, and words actions: so, therefore, one must be very careful of thoughts as well as words and actions. Words of double meaning are very injurious to purity, and no pure woman will speak them, or allow another to do so in her presence.

It is very sad to hear of any woman losing this purity of heart and mind, for once lost it can never, never be recovered, and she is like a valuable vase that has been broken: she can never be the same again.

A woman pure in heart and soul is respected by all her friends and even her enemies, and her life is as good in the sight of God as some of the grandest characters in history.

In conclusion, I would once more say, let your purity be your pride; let it be above all price, even life itself. For life, fame, and riches are nothing without it.

M. H. G.

Modesty and purity are closely allied, and yet there is a dividing line. Slang expressions, loud talk and laughter that attract attention may become habitual to the girl placed in rough environments; and although these cannot be termed symbols of modesty, this same girl may feel a greater hesitancy in disrobing or performing necessary functions of the body before spectators than the girl who is more refined in speech and deportment.

We all remember how as children and young girls, we shrank from exposing a portion of our skins. It was hard to go to the dressmaker even, and uncover arms and shoulders. The instinctive action of hiding any nude part if someone should unexpectedly enter our room; the blush that a personal remark, a bold look, word, or touch will bring to our cheeks, tells us that our integrity has been offended.

It is hard in our crowded flats and apartments to be so very careful of these little points, but I

think it can be done, and we need
to be very watchful if we want
to preserve the sweetest trait in
woman—true modesty.

Is it, then, too late for us older
girls who have grown accustomed
to more or less exposure before
mothers and sisters, alas! often before fathers and brothers—who
have grown so accustomed to hearing the rough jest on the street,
and in the store and factory, that
our faces do not betray the shock—
is it too late to cultivate this trait?
Not one of us but longs for our
young girlhood, when our thoughts
were innocent, our hearts un-
spotted from the world. We cannot unsee or unhear what we have
seen and heard, but I would fain
be glad for the experience that will
help us to understand our fellow-
sisters, and teach us to guard sa-
credly the tender young girls.

There is another form of modesty which adds much to woman's
grace—I mean that which forbids
self-confidence, arrogance and
presumption.

How, then, does modesty differ from purity? Modesty is *purity of manners*, and although this may be sullied by a girl's indecent language, behavior, or dress, and is a dangerous step down to impurity, she may still rigidly preserve her virtue, her virginity.

I can only touch upon this subject; it is too deep for me. How precious to know that from the tiniest flaw of immodesty down to the dark blot of impurity, the repentant heart will be washed whiter than snow in God's sight!

B. W. M.

CHAPTER III.

MARRIED AND SINGLE LIFE.

EFORE discussing whether marriage is a success or failure, I think it would be well to understand what the original designs of the Creator were about marriage, as it is set forth in the Bible : that marriage was the sweet and blessed companionship in life, and the congenial soul union of man and woman. When the man and woman take upon themselves vows and promises which can only, properly speaking, end with the death of one of the parties, it is as solemn as interesting.

Both are inexperienced in the ways of the world, and equally

ignorant of the trials and tribula-
tions of the life before them, and
yet both are so confiding and
trusting, and so full of hope, anticipation, and joy, that it seems
to them nothing can ever shake
their settled bliss.

The success of marriage depends largely upon the internal
attitude and external conduct of
the wife; more so than upon all
other influences combined, for it
requires attention, care, prudence,
watchfulness, foresight, quick in-
tuition, and good, strong common
sense to make marriage a success
through a long term of years.
Our happiness in the married life,
and the success or failure we
make of marriage, must very
largely depend upon ourselves,
let our surroundings and companions be what they may. As marriage is considered in society the
chief end and aim of woman,
ought we not to find mothers in-
stilling into their children self-
respect, self-denial, thought for
others, lessons in kindness and

charity, thoroughness in everything, and to feel that every sacrifice she makes should be willingly and cheerfully done? for
family life will claim some little
sacrifice every day. It is only
thus that true love can exist, for
wherever the spirit of selfishness
is allowed to take its place, discord
will assuredly follow. In married
life, as in everything else, there
must be a correct beginning, and
this is made when the man and
woman who are to make up the
home receive their first training
in early childhood. In most of
the cases where marriage has
proved a failure, an investigation
will show that the man or woman,
or perhaps both, have never received a proper domestic training,
and that each has relied on the
other to make him or her happy.
This very fact alone is fatal to
happiness. The very idea of a
man or woman sitting down and
waiting to be made happy by the
other, and because he or she does
not make the required amount of

happiness, declare marriage a failure, and seek a divorce, so easily obtained!

A girl whose natural domestic tastes have been carefully and properly trained, whether at the Club or in the home circle, strives to make the home the most attractive of all places to her husband, and to carefully study his needs and moods, with an earnest aim to strengthen and help him with all the patience and charity that her nature is or can be made capable of. No girl who may some time take her place by a man's side to become his comforter and helper in fighting the battles of life, and become the mother of his children, the mistress of his home, can begin too early to know all there is to know of domestic duties. There are many unhappy homes where the husband and wife openly declare marriage a failure simply because the wife does not try to become better acquainted with the husband, and *vice versa*. In my

opinion, marriage is a grand success, and the more mutual love
marriages there are, the better
for the community at large. Men
and women are not marrying as
fast as is good and healthful for
public morality and social virtue.
Pure, happy, virtuous homes constitute the nucleus of both Church
and State, and a peaceful, united
pair is the only normal divinely
established unit of humanity, and
the only true center and source of
all that makes life valuable or
earth blessed.   M. J.

Dear girls, let us think back to
the time before we became members of the Society, and recall
what our views on matrimony
were then.

Day after day, week after week,
year after year, the same routine
of work which grew to be drudgery, with but few happy diver-
sions to break the monotony,
made us morbidly long for a
change. To what did our
thoughts most frequently turn?

What was the substance of our day-dreams? Who dwelt in the air castles we built over and over again? Was it not the lover— the husband, who would release us from bondage and henceforth labor and provide for us? How our foolish hearts would flutter as we pictured him asking the one great question! How proud we felt as we walked into the work-room one day with something shining on our left hand that had not shone there before, and how important we felt as we grew to be the center of curiosity, alas, often envy!

All this only in fancy for us who are here to-night, which fancy was too frequently fed by sensational novels. It is a sad truth that too many brides forget the seriousness of the marriage tie, and think chiefly of the change from labor to supposed ease.

But how is it with us *now*, since we have become Club members? Oh, the happy, happy change that came with our initiation!

At last we found a place where we could spend pleasant evenings. Pretty rooms, music, dancing reading, laughter, all help to throw off the burden of the day, and we return home rested and cheered, and surprised to find we could be so young and gay.

Best of all are our practical talk evenings, our Three P Circle. Little by little we learn to look at life from a different standpoint. The interchange of ideas, the sweet, confidential, earnest talk opened new channels of thought, or roused into activity what had been slumbering in our minds; helped us to understand what had been but vaguely felt before.

So with matrimony. We know now that the tender, yet strong and sweet passion given us women is to be kept only for the one whose queen we are to be, and who will return our love in the same full measure. This is the first step to be sure of. Many others must be considered. Can the prospective· husband support a home and the

little ones that may come to bless
it? Is he well? Are we well
and strong enough to take this
step? When we were younger
we too often forgot that marriage
meant motherhood, fatherhood.
Just here lies the fact of greatest
importance which suggests new
and momentous questions: What
of his ancestors? What of ours?
Were there any evil habits, ill
health, on either side, that hered-
ity may hand down to our children? Is our lover pure and
good? Are our lives such that we
need not fear to transfer aught
but good to our offspring? All
this must be carefully considered
before we can conscientiously,
safely, enter this sacred, blessed
relationship.   B. W. M.

When it is the lot of woman to
live single or unmarried, it is only
right to give the greatest thought
to the advantages of such a life,
for there are advantages, though
they may seem only negative.
For one thing, a single woman

preserves more independence of action and more self-reliance of character. One can say, " Yes, I will do so or so," or, " No, I will not do so or so," instead of, " Well, you know, I can't say until I hear what my husband says," which is, of course, quite right when it is remembered that the husband generally supports his wife and children. How often a mother must do violence to her own sense of right, where a child is concerned, because papa says so, and papa is head—often, alas, a perverted one.

A single woman, who earns her own living, let it be ever so scanty, has the comfort of expending the amount she earns as she thinks best. Any shortage falls on herself, who can bear the self-denial, whereas if a woman is married and her husband earning a sufficient income to get along comfortably, the man often monopolizes the largest share of the money, and when the wife wants a little more either for household use or personal expenses, or for the children's need, she is told, " I earn the money and I cannot allow such extravagance." Then the *happy* wife sighs, and wonders why girls are so foolish as to marry. And what responsibility we single women escape in the care of children! We are not tied down and our world hemmed in by Papa, Willie, Johnnie, Katie, and Baby. We are not kept to the grindstone of breakfast, dinner, and supper, making and mending, or sitting up nights with Baby teething, or Johnnie with the mumps, and then being told by Hubby in the morning that he will have to look out for a young wife. No going out evenings, because Hubby goes alone. He can't be bothered with waiting till all the children are in bed, and then, too, he couldn't have as good a time if wife was along. We single women can go anywhere we choose, provided we have our pocketbooks and night key and (as of course we all do) behave ourselves properly.

There is always a cousin or brother
or old friend if one really desires
male escort, but for a real good
sociable time, give me a tried and
true woman friend ; and if she is
a married woman how she will enjoy being with the girls, no matter
if the girls are a little out of their
teens.

It isn't half bad to be an " old
maid." There are always younger
sisters or brothers or nieces or
nephews or little cousins to keep
us sweet and loving, and one need
not be a sour " old maid." Lov
ing a little child is one of the best
investments of affections there is :
you will always get more in the
same coin than you give, and you
can love without the fret and
worry that the poor married
woman is almost always a victim
to. Who is it that is always called
on to take care of the sick, and
does it, too? Florence Nightingale and a host of others. No
longer ago than our late war, it
was mostly " old maids" who
braved the horrors of the hospital

tents, and our trained nurses and
noble Sisters of Charity are almost
without exception single women ;
so hurrah for us!   M. S.

CHAPTER IV.

FAMILY LIFE.

 FAMILY is a group of people bound to each other by ties of blood, known by the same name, and having common interests in life. The family life dates back to the creation of Adam and Eve, and so has God himself as its beginning. We all have a pretty good idea what the true family life requires —care and love one for another, making sacrifices sometimes when needed.

The newspapers are full of unhappy homes, yet there are thousands of happy homes whose histories are never told, and who keep their joys and sorrows to

themselves. Family life is far
from what it ought to be, yet see
how much unselfishness is shown
in nearly every home. Sometimes it would be better if there
were a little less devotion and sacrifice. Instances have been known
where the mother took too much
care and responsibility on herself,
and so made the husband weak
and careless. Sisters have given
up educations so the younger
children could have a longer time
at school.

People cannot live together
without having some of their
sharp corners smoothed down.
Men and women living alone become queer, full of odd ways:
they have no human looking-glass
in their rooms.

When you say "Family Life,"
do you mean starting with the
bride and groom? Of course I
have seen a great many brides, and
how their families grow up in
either happiness or misery. They
start loving each other and meaning to start life doing their duty,

but married life is not always full of sunshine; there are sometimes storms which you must go through, and if the wife is a sensible woman she can often bring the sunshine sooner.

There are cares which the woman alone must bear, but if her choice of a husband is a man willing to help and cheer her, he will brighten her life to such extent that her cares will be forgotten in fond companionship with her husband.

Years ago my father cut the following out of a German paper. It is "A Mother's Advice," to her daughter who is about to become a bride.

"You now go forth into the world to live with a husband you do not know, and leave your parents' roof to make a home for yourself and your husband, and it depends on you what kind of a home you will have.

"When your husband leaves you in the morning to go to business, say 'good-by' in a fond way, that he may be anxious to see

your face in the evening, and when
he comes home don't greet him
with all the trouble and care you
had during the day with help or
with children, or whatever it may
be, for if you do it is not likely
you will receive the sympathy
you expect, as he perhaps has had
some trouble and worry during
the day and will look to you to
make him forget it. For that
reason wait until he is rested and
has his supper, and then if you
think he ought to know it tell
him, and if he is what he ought to
be he will fully sympathize with
you."

This mother further says: "Do
little trifles that you know he will
like, and when he is happy be also
happy, and when he is sad don't
laugh; and, above all, never be contrary, and if you do this you have
done all to make marriage a success, and it will not be your fault
if it is not so."

And when the little children
grow up around you, try to remember that you had liked your
mother to pet and humor you
sometimes, and when they bring

their little cares to you don't snub
them, but sympathize with them;
otherwise, as they grow older they
will find other companions that
will seem to feel more with them,
and by degrees they will become
as strangers in their own homes,
afraid to ask advice where perhaps now it would be willingly
given.

Girls will very often carelessly
hurt their mother's feelings,
whom they can never thank or
repay enough for all the trouble
and care they have made her in
sickness and in health. Think
what she suffered when you were
born, but how quickly it is forgotten in the hope that you will
grow up a blessing and a help to
her. And when you were sick
how she would stay with you day
and night, nursing you without
any complaint, only praying for
your recovery. You can never do
enough for her. She will try to
shield and protect you from all
danger. For that reason don't go
to strangers for advice; go to your

mother, she will tell you right; and if you should have to go to some employment, don't go away cross if you get up a little late, or something went wrong. But say good-by to mother, as some accident may befall you, and the mother will be happy to know that you said good-by with good feeling, hoping to meet again.

And if you have companions that mother does not approve of, do not think she does not want you to have your friends, or wish you to go out, for she has had more experience, and knows what friends are not good for you. .

If children will love their parents and obey them, and love their sisters and brothers, even if little differences will occur they will soon be forgotton in happy thoughts for some little favor, and the welfare of their family will always be their first consideration. Such is my idea of family life.

Rich or poor, every family can be happy in sickness or health

if each and every one tries to
lessen the others' burdens.

E. R.

I think the subject for to-night,
viz., "Can we Influence Brothers
and Sisters?" a very interesting
one, and would like to send this
little message to you. I am
sorry to say I do not think I have
been much of an example to the
younger members of my family.
I have done many things I would
not like to see my younger sister
do; but what I want to tell you of
is a lesson I learned in experience,
and one I hope to remember as
long as I live. I was about nineteen years old, and I was keeping
house for my widowed father. I
left everything neat and clean,
and had gone out to do my marketing, for it was Saturday night,
and in Scotland that means a
pleasant evening for everyone, for
we have a half holiday all the
year round. When I returned, my
brother had the kitchen strewn
with shavings, and tools thrown

all around; you would have
thought it was a carpenter's shop.
I felt so provoked I could have
boxed his ears, and was going to
scold when the thought of what I
saw at the corner stopped me.
It was a crowd of boys; some,
I knew, had been my brother's
schoolmates. They were lounging
around, smoking and cursing and
cutting up, as we so often see at
almost every corner. As I passed,
I thought, what a pity those boys
cannot find something better to
do! I cannot tell you how proud
I felt of my brother that night.
I would have rather cleaned a
thousand times after him than
seen him with those boys. Since
then my father and brother have
never heard me say an angry word
about their making the kitchen a
workshop. Indeed, I have often
found great pleasure in helping
them. I have had great fun saw-
ing and planing wood, and I am
glad I have learned how to glue
and drive a nail. Girls, try to
help your brothers and you will

find great pleasure in doing so. Try and make the evenings pleasant for your younger brothers; from fourteen to eighteen is a very trying time; they have not much spending money, and the dime museum and cheap show are great temptations. Try and plan a little treat for them and companions once a week; a plate of ice cream, a hot soda, a pan of taffy, or a new game don't cost much, but what a good time they give. Remember, it is the little things that count. You can often have a better time from spending fifty cents than five dollars. In conclusion, watch your words, for they can bless like the warm, glad sunshine, and brighten a lonely life; or they can cut in the strife of anger like an open two-edged knife.   M. Y.

Home happiness.

It depends upon each one of us trying to make it the happiest place for us to be in. The trouble is, we are seldom or never con-

tented with our lot; we are
always wanting something we
know we cannot have. Very
often we have an unpleasant task
to perform in the day, and we
come home with a bad temper at
night, giving sister or brother a
sharp answer, or, I am sorry to
say, our parents, too. We should
make our mother our bosom
friend, to tell all our trials to;
then mothers would understand
their daughters better. There
would then be more unity in our
homes, which would certainly
bring more happiness in them.
So let us try to make them as
happy as possible, if it is merely
by our presence in them.

Happiness depends for the most
part on sympathy; often we find
a household whose members are of
no kin, yet who are living in unity
and happiness. It would therefore seem that wherever we live
we might make a home.

There would be greater happiness if we would remember that

it takes two to make a quarrel;
that the other members of the
family have trials and temptations
to contend with as well as ourselves. Then we need to exercise
as much charity and forbearance
at home as outside, as well as a
little patient forethought. This
means a great amount of self-
control and the letting of the tender feelings in our hearts go out
to those who, underneath all else,
we love the most.

The happiness of home depends
on the love of each member of the
family. One unpleasant member
is enough to make home very unhappy.

Two bears, bear and forbear.
Bear ye one another's burdens
and so fulfill the law of Christ.

The happiness of home depends
upon religion. Where there is
true heart religion, everything else
will follow. Also it depends on
respect, love, sympathy, courage,
patience, cheerfulness, common
sense, and co-operation.

CHAPTER V.

HINTS AS TO EDUCATION AND BOOKS.

Practical education.

ALL education, whether practical or otherwise, serves to broaden perception and expand ideas. Practical talks we enjoy at Thirty-eighth Street Club. These talks deal with subjects that touch us in our everyday life, and interest us because they are so real; as food, dressing, money, etc. Practical means capable of being turned to use or account. Practical education, then,.is such as will fit us for doing the work we have to do in the world.

A girl who expects to marry

ought to learn to cook, to do housework, to sew, etc., not by reading about or seeing these things done, but by doing them herself. A dressmaker must have learned her trade by learning how to sew, cut, and fit, by actually doing such work herself.

Head and hand must learn to work together to give us practical education. The head work is our seeing, our observation, and our judging; the hand teaches the muscles to obey the head, and do the work wanted of us, whether it be making a loaf of bread or making a dress, writing a letter or running a sewing machine.

Certain advantages.

In a world like ours where there is so much competition, and where day after day patents are filed at the Patent Office, making improvements on machinery and other things, thus reducing many trades and affecting others by the shortness of time required for labor, perhaps nothing is more essential and advantageous than a practical education.

And leaving manual labor aside, it is of greater benefit than a college course could be, for while the college girl is appropriate to adorn society and astonish people with her knowledge of literature and Latin, the bookkeeper and cashier is making her way through the world, where everything is so uncertain, and the millionaire of to-day may be a pauper to-morrow.

Of course the college girl can make a very good living, but the positions that she is able to fill are too rare to be of use, while the girl with a practical education can fill any position where intelligence, integrity, and good common sense are the principal factors.

Again, one has to pass severe examinations to enter a college, and then spend the larger part of one's youth in accomplishing what does not always prove most beneficial, while in acquiring a practical education we need not devote such a vast amount of time, nor is it difficult to attain it.

X. Y. Z.

How to cultivate the memory.

Memory is the power of retaining impressions made through the senses, and of reviving them afterward without the originals, and by mental force alone.

We are liable to remember anything when the idea of it arises in our mind that we have had that idea before.

If we wish to remember anything, a good idea is to become interested and have sympathy with the subject, for the mind works best when it is interested. The mind has two very distinct powers: the carrying and the hoarding power. The carrying power is the power we use mostly in school days; it answers very well while we have examinations to prepare for, but when we leave school and lose the examinations, we forget what we have heard or studied.

The hoarding power is the principal faculty, for the mind must be taught how to hoard treasures, and not to carry them. For this reason we must notice what interests us most, and give it closer attention, and by doing so impress it on our minds. We must try and arrange our ideas so they bear on some pet subject of ours, so that one idea may call up another.

We find that there are several kinds of memory : The sensational or parrot memory, the kind that is used mostly by children, that is, repeating an article till they know it without understanding the meaning. We find this is a very poor method, for children or grown persons should be made discontented, until the words have meaning for them, as when a person is repeating a verse they have studied, I do not think they should be prompted by repeating the next word ; they should be given the sense of what follows, and in that way be led to think for themselves.

The main difficulty in remembering is to keep certain articles or events in their proper places. At times we get them all mixed up, and the consequence is our story or poetry or whatever we are repeating is anything but interesting to those who are listening. A good idea is to write out whatever we wish to remember, and to underline the emphatic words, beside the different subjects; then to make a list of how to place them, and carry it with us for a short time, and when we wish to think of a subject and cannot remember correctly, to refer to the slip of paper, which will be a great help, but still compel us to use our memory. When a vivid first impression is once secured, the mind must dwell on the subject before it is allowed to pass out of consciousness. The great art of memory is exercise. Nothing suffers more by neglect or increases more by use than the mind. Those who are wont to converse or read but a few things only, will retain but a few in their memory. The mind is like the limbs, the more it is exercised the stronger it grows.

Many people appear forgetful through not having confidence in themselves. How often we see a person lock a door, then run back to see if it is locked, and say, "I thought it was locked." This comes from not putting our mind on what we are doing.

It is the same in spelling words. We know how to spell the word, and still we ask how to spell it, especially when we are writing letters. Then we hear people say, "I know I shall forget it," and instead of grasping what they want to remember, they forget it by their want of confidence in themselves. What is called poor memory is lack of confidence or attention in most cases.

Try to put your mind solely on the subject you have in hand. It is a good plan to imagine you will be called upon to give a description of what you have seen or heard. A. L.

In the first place, it is not an easy matter to cultivate the mind, and I think it is like everything else: it requires a great deal of care and patience, and needs careful training if you expect to derive any benefit from it hereafter.

In cultivating the mind, I would say reading daily papers is one of the best methods that I know of, for the following reasons:

You are interested in current events, and the writers of those papers place everything before you in such a style that you are anxious to know what the result will be next day.

Take plenty of exercise, for if the body is not in good condition the mind may expand, but not be cultivated in a pleasant way. The more you exercise the brain, the easier it is to think and remember things. So long as the body is in a healthy condition, there is no fear of the brain wearing out.

Never worry over anything that is past ; only, use past mistakes or so-called accidents as examples to prevent a recurrence.

I think one of the great mistakes we working girls make is the crowding of so much reading in our half hour for lunch. We hurry over so much matter that we do not allow the brain sufficient time to comprehend clearly the meaning of what we have read.

M. M.

Thoughts about books.

I shall commence by asking you the important question, What books interest you the most? Do novels, books of travel, biographies, or poetry come first in your mind when you are asked this question ? Let us take them separately, and find out which will prove most beneficial to us. But do we read for benefit or for pleasure ? I think even when reading for pleasure we should derive some benefit from it. We will take the inferior novel first, in which the heroine, a poor working girl, marries a duke or lord, and all sorts of delightful things are supposed to happen : have they improved our minds, or are we not rather worse than we were before?   Take a novel of the better class, for instance, one of E. P. Roe's simple love stories, and how much better we feel, and if we stop to think we will find our mind much farther advanced than it would be after reading one of the other books. Books of travel and historical novels open to us delightful scenes in Europe, and in our own beautiful country, and describe them so accurately that when we reach the end we feel as though we had really been there ; perhaps we might never have known of them if we had never read that class of book.

Next come biographies, lives of men and women, many of whom have started on the lowest rung of the ladder, and by patience, perseverance, and ambition have reached the top.   Do we not feel that what others have done before can be done again ?

What shall I say about poetry ? Who, when reading the beautiful lines of poetry, have not wished they could reach the height the poet has attained, and felt something within them stirring in unison with the poet's thought? Books were written for the improvement of our minds and to help us advance in the world, and if we do not read what is proper for us, how can we hope to accomplish it ? Books can also be used to develop a good memory, but to do this we must read a book carefully, not read one page, skip two, and then look in the back to see how it ends, and imagine that we know what is in the book. We can cultivate an interest for good reading by starting with Miss Alcott's delightful books. Do we ever realize what an important part books play in our lives, and how necessary they are to us ?

B. G., Junior.

CHAPTER VI.

HOW TO CULTIVATE GOOD MANNERS.

THERE are many ways in which one can show to those around one that one would be courteous and of good behavior. One especially might be named: that of showing a kindly disposition to those around us, sympathizing with each other in the many troubles and trials of life; and this will lead us to be gentle and patient, and thus our bearing toward those with whom we come in contact will partake of the inward feelings that control us. Never speaking harshly when irritated, or, in other words, controlling ourselves, will also cause us to conduct ourselves in a becoming way.

Good companions have very much to do with good manners. I think there is no truer saying than that " Evil communications corrupt good manners"; so it be-hooves us to guard against bad associations, seeking only those whose example is worthy in some respects of imitation, bearing in mind that if we follow the Golden Rule of our Master, " Do unto others as ye would that they should do unto you," our actions will show gentleness and courtesy to all. M. F.

Good manners, to my way of thinking, is one of the defini-tions of the Golden Rule. Do-ing unto others as you would that they should do unto you is the foundation of good man-ners.

Happily for us, it is free for all to cultivate them, and it is one of the few things that money cannot buy.

Good manners are made up of little things, that taken separately seem very insignificant, but put together make a very large whole. The words "please" and "thank you" are small, but give much pleasure, and make things seem lighter and easier to do. A pleasant smile is often long remembered, and a cordial handshake gives one new life and courage, and the feeling that one has a friend.

The tongue, the little member that can cause so much mischief, can also do wonders in the way of making life pleasant.

Then the small kindnesses that no one sees; the smoothing away of little embarrassments caused sometimes by shyness, awkwardness, or peculiar or ill fitting clothes, which may cause remark. Guarding those around you from any little sharp speeches or unkind remark, never repeating them; and, by speaking well of them, bringing their good points forward; trying as far as you can to make people feel at ease with you at all times.

Meet frankly and as a matter of course the trifling annoyances (for the trifles cause the most trouble) that crop up in our daily life, doing the best we can under the circumstances. These are a few of the things we must habitually practice to have what are considered good manners.

The ingredients for good manners are : respect, love, consideration, thoughtfulness, politeness, tact, and common sense. Mix well until all are smoothly blended and use with discretion.

A. and I. T.

Before we can cultivate good manners, we must understand in what good manners consist. Good manners consist in paying due deference to the aged and infirm, and to those who are in a manner our superiors ; in not being too anxious to air our opinions, in deference to those who are more experienced and consequently wiser than we, though we may not think so; in the "please," for a favor asked, and the "thank you," for the favor granted, and in numberless other little courtesies which make up our daily lives.

Some people seem to have been born with good manners which never desert them. Others have two sets, one for home and one for company. The latter set they put on with their best clothes, to receive, or shall I say deceive? the company. Others, again, have no manners at all, except very bad ones, and they do not seem to care very much whether they have or not. These are the people who constantly shock us, and make us wonder where or how they were brought up.

It does not follow, however, that ill-mannered people are necessarily ill-natured. The worst mannered people are sometimes overflowing with good-nature. They are the people who overwhelm us in a crowded car, in a tone loud enough for everybody to hear, with questions regarding the health of different members of the family, and probably ask questions of a more private nature in the same tone, until we wish we might crawl under the seat, or escape anywhere from that dreadful tongue. Their intentions probably were good, but oh, how woefully deficient in good breeding they were.

Thoughtlessness is the greatest barrier to good manners. If when tempted to say or do a rude thing, we would only stop to think how the action looked, or the word sounded in people's eyes and ears, we might save ourselves and others much annoyance, and tone them down, so that instead of making a bad impression regarding our manners, we might make a good one.

Good manners play a considerable part in our lives. Take, for instance, two people applying for the same position, both equal in intellect and with equal business

abilities. You will find in nine
cases out of ten the one who has
the most prepossessing manners
will be the one accepted to fill the
position, though the other in a
way was just as capable.

But the best way, in my mind, to
cultivate good manners is by having the desire to please people.
When we make up our minds to
do that, we certainly desire to show
ourselves in the best possible light.
We know that being courteous is
pleasing, and perhaps before we
are aware our manners insensibly
improve, simply because we have
the wish to please, and want people to think well of us, which they
cannot do if our manners are de-
fective. If bad manners come
from ignorance, would it not be
well to take somebody whose courtesy and good breeding we admire,
as an example, and try in a measure to become like that?

Mothers and the elders in a
family should be the ones to train
the children in good manners.
The younger a child begins to

learn, the more readily it acquires the habit of true politeness and courtesy; but I am very much afraid we Americans do not think as much about teaching our children politeness as we ought.

M. R.

CHAPTER VII.

JEALOUSY—WHAT IS IT?

TO give a definition for this wretched feeling is impossible, but I will try and tell how it seems to me, and what I have observed in my own life and that of others.

What is it? It is envy, selfishness, and suspicion, to begin with. It is the sweetness of love turned into vinegar of bitterness. A jealous spirit is very sensitive and resentful, and will hunt up bad motives for the purest action. A jealous person loves, but that love means receiving, not giving up. Well, a person shows his character by the love he is capable of having.

Some people inherit jealousy;

how do others get the seeds of this
evil? Might as well ask how did
evil get into the world, anyway.
Of course jealousy is found in all
ranks and conditions of life—between man and wife, among children, among friends, in the workroom, among club members even.
The result is unjust judgment,
fault finding, and general unhappi-
ness. So much for an abstract
view of the subject.

Let me illustrate what has come
under my own observation: A
man who has made himself, wife,
and children miserable by his jealous temper. He certainly loves
his wife, but cannot bear to have
her waste her affection on anyone
but himself. When the children
were small he would begrudge
them the caresses that a mother
loves to bestow on them. When
company comes he will watch with
frowning looks when the wife looks
bright and speaks pleasantly with
them, and after they have gone
will scold and act unpleasantly.

In the workroom the jealous

ones are always fancying themselves slighted, their good qualities and good works undervalued,
and so on. In the clubroom the
jealous ones are not appreciated.
They take pleasure in finding
fault, and stir up bad feeling.

But enough of this. We all
know what it is, have all seen it,
and thought what a bad thing it
was in *other* people. It is all very
well for us to sit here and quietly
talk and give beautiful advice
concerning it, but it takes more
than words to overcome an evil
passion. Much may be done by
not fostering this evil or giving
cause for it. It can be fought as
other evils have been conquered.
Wise friends may give help.
Mothers may do much to give the
crooked nature a straight growth.
Club officers may be cautious and
not give occasion for jealousy.

To entirely uproot this evil
plant takes more than all this:
strength out of weakness—how
can it be infused? Answer, ye
wise ones; I am powerless to

teach others when I know so little of myself. Each one must work out his own salvation. A. M.

Jealousy, and what it is, is a subject I never thought much about, but my opinion is that it expresses a fear that we will lose something which someone else will get, and I will now try and illustrate how a person may become jealous.

There are two girls; one is engaged to a young man; by and by she becomes suspicious that her lady friend is trying to win the affection of her lover, and a fear will come over her that she will lose him, and she is jealous, when perhaps her friend has only a kindly feeling toward him. All this feeling could have been avoided if the girl had been more kindly, and less selfish in her feelings toward her lady friend. But I think that every person at some time during his life experiences jealousy, but in different ways. It may be something very small, and you try not to be jealous, but we may have a very dear friend whom we love very much. If sometimes they pay more attention to others we are apt to feel a little jealous and to feel, Oh, she does not care as much for me as she used to. But if we love persons very much we cannot expect them to speak to us always and to give up everyone else for us; we occasionally meet such people. Or a person may be praised for something we ought to be praised for also. If we do not receive the praise, we feel as if we had a right to, and so become jealous. Others would not care, but feel rejoiced to have their friends praised.

If we would just think a little more good-naturedly, and try and make an excuse for them, how much better we would feel, for jealousy brings discontent.

Sometimes you will see it about a girl's looks. One will say, "Don't you think Angeline is pretty?" and the other will say,

"Oh, I don't think so." Then they will say, " Oh, she is jealous." And in many other ways you can be jealous. Some people are jealous all the time. They can't bear to see anybody have anything, but want all themselves, and become jealous if the person gets along better than they.

We often wonder how the feeling comes. I think if we would not let things like that bother us we could avoid a good deal of jealousy.   I. T.

I think we girls should know more than anybody else what jealousy is, for we are in the midst of it every day. Whether it be in the workroom or our Club the air seems to be full of it, yet we all deny it when we are accused of being jealous of anything, so it must be something that we feel ashamed of. We don't like to own up to that fear which makes us uneasy when we think of some- one robbing us of the affections of those we love, or that she is likely to enjoy some advantage which we desire ourselves, though it burns within us all the same.

And if our expected rival should succeed, we are almost sure to feel full of envy, which is a miserable feeling; so we may well ask ourselves the question how to avoid jealousy. Now I don't think anybody, if she would confess fairly, would say she never remember being jealous. Yet it makes me, who often feel that way, wish I could think of something to avoid that feeling; but I am afraid I will always have a little of it breaking out in spite of my desire to suppress it. I may take a different view when I get older, but what I have seen and what little I have read about it, makes it seem a disease we are all afflicted with more or less, as it comes out in so many different ways. I think it would be foolish for me to attempt to describe the different kinds of jealousy there are in the world, for I feel sure to do so would fill a very large book.

And after that book was filled
I would find so much jealousy
left out that I would have to begin again.

But I suppose you only wish
to hear of jealousies that trouble
us girls most, and how to try to
avoid them. Well, I hear a girl
talk of being jealous of some
young man that she thought was
very attentive once, but not quite
so much now. Well, poor girl, I
am sorry for her if she caught his
attention in the right way, but in
most cases I think it is the girl's
fault, and if she had only conducted herself properly she would
have saved herself that feeling.

I have never had a sweetheart
of any kind yet, but suppose I
may have one some time. Remember, I am only supposing, and
he happens to be just the kind
I've been dreaming about; not one
of those fellows that stand at
street corners in groups, that has
something to say to every girl that
goes by, and spends all his money
in a saloon and on cigarettes. If

you get jealous about one of those fellows, your mother had better lock you up quickly. I mean one that is manly, that you get introduced to in the right way, by some friend that you have a right to have confidence in ; and suppose I learn to like him very much, but by and by I hear of or see him paying some attentions to that stuck-up one over the way that does not know how to mend her own stockings; will any of you dare to say to me, " Lucy, don't be jealous " ? No, it can't be done. You may tell me some way that would help me to feel not so bad about it, but I could not avoid being jealous.

L. D., Junior.

Jealousy is the green-eyed monster, as it is sometimes called, and one of the most evil passions of which the human heart can be guilty. In its worst form it is a species of insanity, and through its influence many crimes have been committed and numerous lives ruined.

Children in one family are sometimes jealous of a brother or sister.
They think that he or she, which-
ever the case may be, receives
more love from the mother than
the rest, and they make the life of
the supposed favorite miserable
whenever a chance presents itself ;
but let one of the jealous ones fall
sick or be in trouble and he will
soon find that one child is just as
dear as another to the mother,
and each shares equally in her
love.

Perhaps we have a friend whom
we have always considered as our
especial property. She makes a
favorable remark concerning another girl, and in a moment we are
up in arms, ready to defend our
rights (we want no poachers).
The flaws we can find in that girl's
looks and disposition in about two
minutes are simply wonderful.
She would never recognize herself
in the picture we portray of her,
and woe betide her if we ever meet
her: she will surely feel the might
of our jealousy and anger, though

she is entirely ignorant of having aroused any such feelings in us.

Jealousy is only another name for selfishness. We are not willing to share the affections of those we love with others. We want all or nothing, and in the end, if we allow this selfish feeling to have its way we get nothing. Of all the wretched people in this world, those having a jealous disposition are most wretched. They are miserable themselves, and they make those whom they love, and who love them, miserable by an unreasonable jealousy.

There are people (without a conscience, perhaps), who, knowing a person is afflicted with a jealous disposition, take delight in arousing that jealousy. If they only knew what misery they were breeding for the jealous one, I think they would think twice before arousing a passion whose consequences are usually so disastrous. M. R.

CHAPTER VIII.

PRACTICAL MATTERS.

Money and its use.

THE value of money is only to be judged by its possessors, who use or abuse it according to the value they place upon it.

Its value when used properly is beyond estimate, while abused it causes many innocent hearts to ache with pain and misery ; it fills our prisons with criminals, and brings countless numbers to untimely ends.

When given in a worthy cause the value of money can be appreciated by the lightened hearts and cheerful faces it occasions. Also as a means of relieving distress it

is a pearl beyond price. In need
we realize its necessity and recognize its virtues.

What is the value of a five-
dollar gold piece? That depends
upon who has got it, and how the
owner obtained it. If a child has
it in its little hand, and thinks of
all the Christmas presents it wants
to buy, it may seem like a fortune.
If a South Sea Islander had the
gold piece, it would merely be a
pretty piece of metal—for a sav-
age has very few wants, and needs
no money.

If a Club girl has the gold coin,
she may go to Holiday House (if
it is summer time) and get the
full value of her money.

Each one sets a value upon
money according as it is obtained.
If I work hard for my money, I
will be more careful in spending
it than if someone made me a
present of it, or I got it through
the Louisiana Lottery. Some
people overestimate the value of
money.

Samuel Smiles, in his book on

Thrift, in speaking on this subject, says, "Money by itself can do nothing. The Apostle Paul planted the knowledge of the Christian religion over half of the Roman Empire, yet he supported himself by tent making, and not by collecting subscriptions."

Some people undervalue money. Poor people think because they have so little it is no use to save ; if they had more, perhaps it would be worth while. And yet we read in the newspapers of street beggars getting from three to five dollars a day, from the small sums so easily collected. Many of the best qualities of one's character are brought out in knowing how to use money rightly : as forethought, generosity, justice, and benevolence. Bad traits are developed in the wrong use of money, as extravagance, greed, and dishonesty.

It is great wisdom to understand the true value of money and how best to use it. Some

learn by experience, and some are
spendthrifts all their lives.

Sure use alone,
Makes money not a contemptible stone.
—*George Herbert.*

Money is power throughout the
world. With it you are envied
and flattered by almost each individual whom you come in contact with. You will have friends
by the dozen who will willingly
help you spend it as long as you
pay their way, but let them know
your funds are running low, and
your "summer friends" have no
further use for you.

There are very few things in
this world which money cannot
buy; even, we have read a con-
demned criminal can have his
sentence revoked if there is money
to back him. The only things
which I can think of that cannot
be bought are Life, Death, Health,
and Happiness.

Money is in nine cases out of
ten at the root of all evil, and how
many girls who are leading a

wrong life to-day, can trace their downfall to the want of more money for style, and that means living beyond your means; but more of that later.

Even our yearly elections are supposed to be governed by each man's own principles, but you can always see in the end the candidate who has spent the most money receives the office. Money is put to different purposes, some of them as follows:

The miser loves to hoard it,
The women they adore it,
The only friend a man can have,
Is money on this earth.

How to use it! At the end of a week a girl who has worked receives her salary. Most of us have planned beforehand what we would buy with it, but is it always put to the best advantage by buying a dress or a hat because our friend has one, and it looks so stylish, or buying bargains in the stores which we think we may need later, etc.?

That is not my idea of using money to its best advantage. In building a house men start at the very foundation, and little by little it forms the house. So it is with saving money; you have to start, just as the men do, at your foundation, and by that I mean, look to your pennies and small change. A girl wouldn't think of spending a bill foolishly, but this change—it really is so heavy in her pocketbook she must do something to get rid of it, and therefore loses some material to build with.

Then again you will find girls who think by buying on the installment plan they save their money. They are the ones who also are losing the materials. If your salary be ever so small, put something aside, and if it be only twenty-five cents a week at the end of the year you will have a total of thirteen dollars, a nice sum of money to start your bank account, and if you have started it, your wish to save money will be more developed, and many a thing which you now think you cannot do without will be passed by, and the amount of the purchase will be added to your bank account, and your principal will slowly grow, and your money will be put to a good use.   S. H.

Thoughts as to dress.

Women should dress according to their means, and not go beyond their income for fashion's sake. There is often danger in buying something new because it is the fashion, and when it is not necessary this means extravagance. If women would follow a fashion of kind deeds and good will toward their sisters half as earnestly as they do fashionable dressing, they would find much happiness.

I think people ought to dress according to their means, whether it is the fashion or not. It is a duty that a woman owes to humanity to appear as well as her circumstances will allow, that is, to be dressed neatly, comfortably, and to follow the fashion as long as there is nothing ridiculous in the fashion.

In dress, as in all things, we should learn to use common sense.

Women should study themselves and dress accordingly. No true woman will dress showily or loudly; they rather dress in a quiet, neat way, with everything in harmony. Dress, gloves, hat should match, and everything be of good material, because it will wear better than if it is cheap.

The tendency is still toward extravagant dress, but I think there is a strong tide in the direction of simplicity, comfortable and hygienic dressing, and I think this will last—foolish fashion to the contrary, which will be short-lived. I believe this because American women are too sensible to go back to discomfort after having learned the luxury of simple, healthful dressing.

I think that women should consider their position in the world, and their means. Then these words come in here as regards dress—suitability, neatness, simplicity, economy—a due regard to fashion under subjection to comfort.

Happiness in little things.

Little things have a very great power to make or mar our happiness. Our lives are made up of little things, so also our happiness. It is the little things which help us to make up our estimate of a person's character, and it is the little things of everyday life by which our friends and acquaintances judge us. It depends a great deal upon ourselves whether we are happy or otherwise. If we are determined to look on the bright side, we will soon find a great many little things that will add to our happiness. A bright day, a pleasant smile, a kind word, and little things will contribute to our happiness. It is best to

Always look on the sunny side,
Although life checkered be,
A gladsome heart bids care depart,
And time flies pleasantly.

If, on the other hand, one is inclined to see every little trouble, she will soon see nothing else, and they will appear much greater than they really are from merely thinking of them, and making mountains out of molehills. The best way to be happy is not to think whether you are so or not, but rather by being on the watch for the little things to add to the happiness of others.   B. M.

We all have our trials and temptations, some of which we make for ourselves, while others come from outside sources. Some days seem all sunshine, others are all clouds; and the clouds and sunshine are in a measure chiefly of our own making.

For example: It is Monday, and a very blue Monday perhaps for some of us. We get out of bed probably the wrong way, and the clouds are dull, and our faces and spirits match the clouds; before leaving home we say something cross to the mother and make her feel badly, and we go our way with the feeling of irritation against ourselves for having done so. All day long things go wrong, and it seems as though everybody had conspired against us to make life unendurable. We look for the fault in others, when in reality it lies in ourselves.

When night comes, glancing back over the events of the day, we say to ourselves, What a wretched day this has been! To-morrow I will try and keep my temper, and exercise a little patience with those around me. The next day probably the skies are no brighter than on the day preceding, but with our resolution kept bravely before us the trials and annoyances which seemed so great the day before sink into nothing when the resolve we have made of keeping our temper, and exercising patience is brought to bear upon them.

Why is it we cannot always remember that every trial cheerfully borne and every temptation bravely resisted but teaches us greater patience to endure those which will follow? If life were all smooth sailing, when the great trial of temptation came to us, as it must come some time in our lives, where would we find the reserved strength and patience to meet it? I. T.

CHAPTER IX.

INFLUENCE OF ART UPON LIFE.

THE influence of art upon our lives. When we speak of art we usually mean painting, sculpture, music, and the drama. What good do pictures do us? In a beautiful picture the artist has arrested and captured and fixed forever on his canvas the beautiful object, so that we may have it forever before our eyes, and look at it as often as we desire to, and gratify to the fullest extent that sense of the beautiful that we all have, and thereby become nobler, if only in our own thoughts and for the moment, for it seems to me nothing beautiful can be bad, and

therefore must be good; sin is
the great destroyer of beauty.
Who has not come back from a
visit to our Metropolitan Museum
of Art, broadened and ennobled,
and with his sense of the beautiful keenly sharpened? I think
very few of us. Pictures are a
most valuable factor in one's education. With how many persons,
scenes, and places have they made
us familiar, which we would have
otherwise known little about!

To my mind sculpture teaches
us repose and proportions. If our
modern young woman would only
realize how very beautiful some
of the famous female figures are,
and how they were appreciated
and immortalized ages ago, she
would probably be induced to let
out her own pretty little Frenchy
waist an inch or two.

Music is probably the thing
that appeals to us with more force
than anything else. How far and
away out of ourselves the strains
of a violin takes us, and how the
roll and swell of a grand organ

seems to quiet and soothe us, and
send our thoughts heavenward;
and in this busy world of ours,
with its impatient haste and mad
rush, these little moments of being
calmed and soothed count for a
great deal. I have known even
the much despised hand organ to
effectually drive away a fit of the
blues with a few bars of its bright
dance music. Long live the hand
organ !

Lastly comes the art of acting.
How easy it would be to remember our history if we could see
the scenes and events acted out
before our eyes, as we have seen
scenes and events of less importance. Acting is another very
important factor in our education,
and reflects the manners and
customs of a given period with
vividness and truth.

Take Shakspere's plays, for instance: no matter how carefully
one may read them, one can never
so well know and understand the
characters and their relation to
each other as when one has seen

them all living on the boards before him.

So the influence of art upon our
lives can be nothing but broaden-
ing and elevating. Art in any
form takes us out of and away
from ourselves, and emphasizes to
us the fact that we are but a very
small atom in the scheme of the
universe.   G. A.

Art is that which by skill has
become a masterpiece, such as
science, ability, profession, trade,
handicraft, cunning, deceit, trick,
and device; fine art is that which
is connected with taste and judgment, and may be divided into
three classes: pictures, statuary,
and architecture. These go hand
in hand with the Muses, music,
poetry, and literature. Then
comes science, which is also a great
art, and may be divided into four:
first, astronomy; second, geology;
third, geography; fourth, agriculture. Then comes house decora-
tions, needlework, and cookery.
By some, cooking may not be con-

sidered an art, but to me it seems an art which every woman, rich or poor, must cultivate if she wishes a healthy, happy household.

Does art influence life? Most certainly it does. We cannot live without it. It is food for the body, mind, and soul. The eye has an appetite for beauty, the ear for a sweet sound, and the mouth for a pleasant taste. To prove this, let us take, for example, the picture of the Madonna bending in holy joy over the Christ Child, or the Emigrants in the Gallery of the Eden Musée, or that of the Roll Call. Let us look earnestly for five minutes at each of these pictures and they will teach us more than we could learn in a volume.

Now we come to statuary. Is it not wonderful that God has given man power to take a huge unshapely stone and create such work as Dante's Hell, or that of the Three Graces? Then comes architecture. As we tread the

sacred courts of the old cathedral,
and look around and above us on
the solid masonry that has stood
the storms of centuries, do we not
feel that we stand indeed upon
holy ground? and while we gaze
in wonderment there steals upon
our ears the sweet and solemn
sound of the organ, now soft
and low, then swelling into
the mighty Hallelujah chorus,
like a peal of thunder, while
in the distance comes the soft
low notes, like the voice of
the Master saying, "Peace, be
still."

We have proved the appetite of
the eye and ear; now we come to
the appetite of the mouth. By
much toil and skill the earth has
been made to produce every necessity of life, but little is ready
for the mouth until it has been
cooked. Should we not then cultivate the art of cooking, which is
the finest touch of the great art
of agriculture, by placing on our
tables not only that which will be
pleasant to the taste, but that

which will preserve in perfect health our bodies, which should be the temples of the living God?

M. Y.

"For anything to influence us we must have the sublime with us," quotes the poet. Now what are generally considered as the arts? I heard an old gentleman say that he considered "Nature's art" the most beautiful. The flowers, trees, and sunsets should have more influence upon life than they have. They should raise more sublime ideas and should always remind us from whence they came. To me, poetry, music, and books compose the most beautiful arts. When I read Tennyson's "May Queen," and Longfellow's "Psalm of Life," and others of his, I receive an impression which I think will always last. I seem to be carried out of myself, and to enter into the poet's idea and soar to the height the poet had obtained. Different natures are affected by different arts. I knew a lady within whom music awoke the best and holiest feelings, while on others it had no effect at all. But does it really influence us, or does it pass off after a time? I think it very often leaves a lifelong impression. I have heard it said by foreigners that Americans were in too much of a hurry for anything to impress or influence them, but I do not think that is so. Why shouldn't we be influenced by the beautiful things around us—to have our thoughts raised to higher objects, and to have our ambitions raised by the arts? Pictures as an art have no influence upon me; I admire them, and think no more about them. Conversation is also considered as an art, and one which I admire very much, and it is also very useful to be able to say just the right thing at the right moment. It is also an art that requires a great deal of study, which seems very strange. Housekeeping can also be considered an art, and I

read in the paper the other day
of a man who considered it an
art to find names for all his
babies.

B. G., Junior.

CHAPTER X.

WOMEN AS MORAL REFORMERS.

T IS not so many years since the direct and personal participation of a woman in any public enterprise was looked upon as unseemly or as unsexing her, according to the spirit of the times. The great temperance and other moral reforms of the first part of this century proceeded without the help of women as active agents. Women, as a rule, contributed their prayers and their influence in domestic life, but they were listeners and not speakers. In the churches women constitute two-thirds of the membership, but the organization of the church is in the hands of men. In the early centuries it was considered disgraceful for a woman to assume to meddle in such matters. It was considered her duty to stay indoors, except where duty absolutely called her abroad; to hold her peace in the house of God, and to cover her head even when she prayed.

When women first began to appear on public platforms, people shook their heads and prophesied degradation for society as the inevitable consequences. Women would unsex themselves, said the critics; they would lose their feminine charms, homes would be neglected, and manners would be roughened. A favorite picture of those days was of the distracted husband tending the baby while the wife was off battling for her rights. Good and conservative people really thought that the disposition of women to exercise their full powers in society, and to attain the fullest intellectual development, was the sign of untold evils to come on the race.

A generation ago it was a rare

and brave girl who ventured beyond the narrow sphere within
which conventionality confined
feminine activity. Now all that
has changed, and the change has
come with surprising rapidity.

The appearance of women as
speakers on public platforms, and
as organizers and directors of
public enterprises, is taken as a
matter of course. Women of social distinction will serve on com-
mittees of the World's Fair at
Chicago. Women commissioners
to that exhibition will be appointed by the Governors of the
States. Clubs and societies of
women discuss questions of public
reform in all parts of the Union.
The present temperance movement is largely, if not chiefly,
in the hands of women, the
Women's Christian Temperance
Union being foremost in the good
work. At political meetings seats
are set apart for women concerned
as to public questions, and there
is hardly a movement, secular or
religious, which starts or proceeds

without calling in the aid of feminine energy.

This introduction of the feminine element into the work of the world, and more especially the work of moral reform, involves a new phase of civilization. It means that the forces of reform are to be strengthened and enlarged to an enormous extent. The half of the race which of old was counted out of such movements, is now to be counted in. Women have thrown off the shackles with which long time customs, conventionalities, and prejudice bound them. They have found out their strength, and they will exert it for the benefit of society. Social opinion and public sentiment do not now stand in the way of their progress, and hence the occasion for their former timidity about taking part in public enterprises has passed away. It looks, therefore, as if we were entering upon a new phase of civilization in which the feminine influence will be powerful everywhere, and with it will come a higher moral tone, a keener and more sensitive moral sentiment, and a profounder sense of moral obligation.

In quiet and unobtrusive ways, in the home and in society, women have always been doing their best to reform individual men. Now, they are extending the sphere of their exertions and seeking to reform all men. They are also working with a tenacity of purpose so great, and with so much intelligent zeal, that they are moving the world by their concerted efforts. Whether the duty of suffrage is imposed upon them or not, sooner or later they are destined to be the chief agents in bringing about the reformation of society, its elevation, and its purification. They have taken the forward steps, and they will not go back. They will move ahead steadily and irresistibly. The "Woman's Age," as a well known writer calls it, is in its beginning only. M. J.

The subject is so large that I can only give the outline as it appears to me in a disconnected way.

What is moral reform? Is it not fighting against evil, and working to promote truth and justice? Neither men nor women can do this work of moral reform alone. They need to work together and help each other.

Perhaps it would be better to ask, What qualities do women possess that make them oftener moral reformers than men? From time to time we have had for our Tuesday evening talks the lives of noted women. A few names might be mentioned, and you will recall the work of moral reform wrought by each. Harriet Beecher Stowe, writing "Uncle Tom's Cabin," and the blow it gave to slavery. Florence Nightingale's work in hospital reform. Dorothea Dix and the insane asylums. The Ohio Women's Temperance Crusade, now so powerful under Frances Willard.

But these women were exceptional women, and what interests us is how can we with no particular mission act as moral reformers. We can no more stop exerting influence on others, either for good or ill, than we can stop breathing, so we *must* work for moral uplifting or moral debasement.

We must begin with ourselves; let our better nature have a chance of development, become strong by resisting temptation, learn self-control. The ways of working are different. Some women work for moral reform by speaking or writing, but perhaps the best way is by living a pure, womanly life.

Why do women work for moral reform? A woman is quick to see, fertile in advice, and strong to protect when those she loves are in danger, or when she sees suffering that she can alleviate. Women work for the safety of home; what would work harm to husband and children she will oppose. Women work for moral reform by working through the Churches—spreading truth and religion throughout the earth. Women's work for the helpless, the poor, the sick, and the aged, tends to relieve misery and make this world a better place to live in.

Men and women who take St. Paul's definition of love, believe in the sanctity of home and marriage, and the obligations of personal purity, are the salt of the earth, working against the corrupting influence of the age.

H. A. J.

Are women moral reformers? We meet with so many different classes of women, and those I come in contact with daily I can say try to do what they can toward moral reformation.

There are some women that can do a great deal more than others. For instance, in factories and in a great many workshops there are some women who by a kind look or a kind word make a great impression, while others doing the same thing do not make any impression whatever. I think when a woman has made an impression on a certain person, that person has taken a liking to the moral one, and tries to do what she can to please her, while for another that she does not like she will do all sorts of mischief to make her angry.

There are times when groups of four or five girls get to talking together, and whatever their conversation may be, if another girl of a more moral disposition than theirs happens to join them, the conversation is instantly dropped, because they have respect for the girl that is morally inclined.

A JUNIOR.

CHAPTER XI.

GLIMPSES INTO THE BUSINESS PART OF LIFE.

A peep into a sewing room.

I FEEL proud to tell you I have spent some of the happiest days of my life in the workroom, and found some of my best friends there. I am sure it was there I finished my education. The whole tenor of our lives depends in a measure on the class of girls we are placed among in the workroom. If we meet the right class of girls, we will try to improve ourselves in every way possible, no matter what our home life may be. One good ambitious girl can do as much good in a workroom as some of our public speakers do abroad. We do not need to lead a public life to be of use in the world, as I have found by many of the characters I have met.

I will try to give you a description of one girl whom I have met, and was attracted toward her by the first glimpse. She had a very sad but sweet face, and I would often sit and wonder who she was and what her trouble could be. I asked several of the girls if they were acquainted with her, but none of them seemed to know her, although she had worked there for some time. I was anxious to become acquainted with her, but did not know how to approach her. I met her on the stairs one morning and saluted her, and from that morning we have been the best of friends.

I found my new friend to be a very intelligent person, and one who had traveled quite some, but her travels were not pleasure trips. We became the best of friends, and walked home together in the evening, and it was then that she told me of her troubles—how her father died, leaving the family without means. She being the oldest child had to help her mother bear the burden; after working all day, she would do another day's work at home, washing and sewing to keep the younger children comfortably dressed.

The second eldest child was a boy, and he was employed in an office. His salary was very small, but they were anxious to give him a chance to raise himself. He was a very bright boy, and advanced rapidly, but when he was old enough to earn a fair salary he got married, leaving herself and mother almost heart-broken. Then they had to struggle on as best they could, and were very much discouraged. It was at this time I met her, and did my best to make her feel at home with some of the girls. I knew if they conversed with her they would find her interesting, and would be likely to become friends. We thought she was lonely, and took great interest in the stories she told of her travels, and we kept her so busy amusing us that she forgot her own troubles.

If we were more considerate how much more happiness there would be in the workroom! Every one of us were better for having met her, and I am sure we will never forget her.

Factory life.

Factory life brings up the old question, Why do people as a rule look down on factory girls?

I will say that from my own experience in the factory, I have met with as lovely girls as I would care to know—girls who have made their lives one sacrifice that would in a measure be a lesson for some of our more fortunate sisters to learn.

Their good influence in the workroom has been felt by both young and old. When I have heard people speak disrespectfully of the factory girl, one cannot imagine my feelings, particularly when I have these bright, self-sacrificing creatures before me; yet I had to keep still instead of defending them, which I could do if the conversation was directed to me.

This is a very deep subject, and I cannot treat it as I should. If people would only look at this subject as they ought, and put themselves in our position, and see if they would make their lives as great a success as we factory girls have, I think that circumstances would alter the case very much. When one thinks of the long hours in a confined, crowded factory, with the din of the machinery constantly grinding on our ears all day long, and so wearing on our nerves, is it a wonder that girls who talk loudly on the streets are classed as factory girls? They are so used to shouting when they do talk in order to be heard above the noise of the machinery, and as it takes time to effect a change, the time between their leaving the factory and appearance on the street is so short, the only way to avoid this will be shorter hours for work and more time for improvement.

I have known girls from twelve years up, who have worked in the factory for ten hours and a half per day, rush home in the evening, eat a hurried supper, and then go to night school. This same thing for six days in the week, and then Sunday comes, the only day of rest. Off to church in the morning—Sunday school in the afternoon, and at this point let me ask what time have these girls for improvement? I am not upholding factory girls simply because I work there, for if I could better my condition I would willingly do so, and I believe that every other factory girl would do the same.

The question arises, Can a conversation such as is intended to elevate be carried on in the factory for any length of time? I say that it is next to an impossibility, as you would have to speak so loud that you would get hoarse in a very short time. The factory girl is considered by some as rude and vulgar, yet when it comes down to practical charity you will find them more than willing to help anyone in need or distress as much as they possibly can. I have met many people outside of a factory, yet when they come to know you are a factory girl it seems to condemn you. Why do these feelings exist? But at any rate they do. Why don't these people who talk about the factory girls so much use a little of their spare time to bring about a change, instead of talking about it? Then I think there would be a great many more happy homes as well as work-rooms, as the girls would have more time to brighten their lives as well as their homes.

One of the greatest advantages of the day for the bettering of working girls, has been the formation of clubs where factory girls meet the teachers, etc., on an equal standing, uniting and bringing their ideas and interests more closely together, cultivating good-fellowship, and meeting people better educated and more fortunate than themselves.

M. G.

The life of a factory girl is, I consider, what she makes it herself. If she does her work properly she will find that her boss uses her with all due respect, and that is a great thing. Then her roommates come next. If she makes as near as possible all things agreeable for them, they in almost all cases do the same for her. As for education, the most of them have a fair share of it. They have to be pretty smart to become good workers, and as far as generosity goes, there is no class that is more ready and willing to help in all instances than the factory girl. Then another thing that goes to make her life pleasant is the accommodation that is in the building. If the factory is large and well kept of course it is more pleasant for her, as the biggest part of her time is spent there.

M. S., a Junior.

Saleswomen and shoppers.

To a close observer the many different types of saleswomen make an interesting study. First you meet the fine lady floor walker, whose manner is so stately one is almost afraid to address her, and when at last you do pluck up courage enough to ask timidly where you will find ribbons, she treats you to a haughty stare, and with an imperious gesture tells you, one room to the right, and dismisses you. When anything annoys her, her wrath descends on the head of the poor little cash girl, whom she is always driving along.

You are relieved to find her opposite type in the young woman who shows you " a love of a bonnet." She is effusive to a degree, and tells you, with a sweet

smile, " My dear, that bonnet becomes you perfectly, and you
don't look a day over seventeen
in it," and more to the same effect. She has evidently had a
close acquaintance with the
blarney stone. But you leave
her well satisfied with yourself,
though perhaps you find when
the bonnet comes home it is not
nearly as becoming as you
thought.

Then you come across the girl
who is so busy talking to her
neighbor about last night's recep-
tion that she does not seem to be
aware that you have asked the
same question several times, and
when for the third time you repeat your question, she looks up
and appears hurt that you should
interrupt her, answers shortly, re-
turns to her friend and begins to
show her the last new waltz step,
while you wait patiently to be attended to.

Next you meet the real cross
girl. She has begun the day
wrong and feels that she cannot

be pleasant if she tried; perhaps she has come away without her breakfast, because she has gotten up too late, and that is enough to make anyone cross. You ask to be shown certain goods, and with a sullen look she spreads the goods before you, and speaks in such a sharp manner that you feel your temper rising.

But think, good people, of all the annoyances the girl behind the counter has to put up with. Think of the many women who shop and ask to have box after box taken down, knowing all the time that they do not intend to purchase anything. Think of all this and keep your temper. Do you wonder that the girls are cross, when their heads are perhaps throbbing or their backs aching, while idle women sit tossing over the goods and giving them unnecessary trouble?

We cannot leave the subject without a glance at the sweet-faced, gentle girl, who looks up with such a pleasant smile. She

is kindly attentive to all your
wants, and makes timely suggestions if you seem to be in doubt.
She never misrepresents the goods
she is selling, and you feel you
can depend on what she tells you;
and when you leave her the world
seems brighter for having met her.
In fact, she is an ideal saleswoman
whom we seldom meet.

L. C.

There are two kinds of shopper—one does it for pleasure or
to pass the time away ; the other
from necessity, so few of us being placed so that we can transfer that duty to another. The
first, although very annoying, we
should feel very sorry for. How
void her life must be when she
has no higher aim than to lounge
about from shop to shop, wearing
out the life of salespeople in
their effort to please her and induce her to buy. The second,
though not less troublesome at
times, is not so from choice. The
special sales and differences in lo-

cation make it necessary to go from place to place.

To shop well we should know what we want before we start. It is a great help to have a memorandum, but even then we cannot always get what we want for the asking, and often get confused and worried to know what is the next best. How helpful it is then to meet a person behind the counter who will take the trouble to think over their stock, or put themselves in your place for a minute, or long enough to make a kindly suggestion, thereby getting the good will of a customer for themselves and the store!

I would suggest politeness and consideration on the part of buyer and seller. It makes life and work go much more smoothly. I do not think there is anything so discouraging to a person trying to get the value of their money as to come in contact with a person who works only for the money they get, having no sympathy with their task, and showing by

their manner that everything and
everybody is a bore, forgetting
that they are acting dishonestly
to their employer by making
people dislike the shop—as one
always feels that the manners of
the clerks is the will of the employer.

I don't think there can ever be
an excuse for indifference on the
part of the clerk, because no matter how often a person goes into
a store without buying they still
do some good as an advertising
medium, they being always ready
to tell those who do want to purchase where they will get best
suited.

I will conclude by advising patience and good temper on the
part of shopper and clerk. Having done a great deal of buying
and selling, I think it is at times
as hard work for one as the other.

M. McC.

*An instance during the busy season
at the hat counter.*

We are in the height of the

busy season at the hat counter;
every customer is anxious to be
attended to at once, and we try
our best to please them and to be
agreeable. Sometimes the confusion is dreadful. Early in the
afternoon a lady comes in with a
little girl; she asks me if I am
busy. I tell her I am, but if she
will wait a moment I will attend
to her. She wants a hat for her
little girl. The mother I can suit,
but with the child that is an impossibility. At last one hat is
found which the mother thinks is
lovely; but the child insists that
"she don't like it; it hurts her
head, and it is a horrid old hat,
anyway." Finally the mother
says, " Well, I'll tell you what we
will do; you put that hat aside
and we will look around and see
if in some of the other stores
we can find anything we like
better." I say, "All right," and
the woman goes after taking
nearly half an hour of my
time.

The hat is still lying on the

counter when another lady and
child come in. The former sees
the hat, places it on the little
one's head, and says, " I think I
shall take this." The child is not
asked whether she likes it or not,
but seems to take it for granted
if her mother likes it, it is all right.
They go out, and I say to myself,
" I wish all customers were like
those."

About a quarter to six the first
lady comes in, the little girl still
with her. Both are flushed and
very tired, and the child is abom-
inably cross. The mother says,
" We have found nothing to suit
us, and I think I shall take that
hat." I say, "Madam, it is sold,"
(perhaps there is a little venom in
the way I say it). Of course she
is angry ; the hat seems very desirable when she cannot have it,
and the child wants that hat, too,
and insists she will have no other.
Finally, I promise to try and get
one exactly like it, and they go
away partly appeased.

Oh, there are shoppers and

shoppers; some we love to attend to, and others we wish we could steer clear of when we see them coming to purchase.

V. R.

CHAPTER XII.

HOW CAN WE HELP ONE ANOTHER?

THE papers read at our second conversation on "What do Working Girls Owe One Another?" show how much alike we are in our ideas of what a working woman should be. All speak of the mutual respect, love, sympathy, truth, loyalty, faith, and oneness of purpose we owe one another, each having her individual duties to perform, and performing the same to the best of her ability; not allowing ourselves to be overcome by the trifles that come into our everyday life as we are so apt to do. We need, too, to realize the honor and nobility of work, and feel proud of it whatever it may be. Being true to ourselves in the first place, for we cannot have the good influence we would like to over those we meet unless we become in a measure what we would like others to become, and by trying ourselves, we are often silently, unconsciously, but surely influencing those around us.

All of this brings us back to the Golden Rule: the putting one's self in another's place; for if we kept the old-fashioned Golden Rule, would we not be loving, sympathetic, loyal, true, having more faith in one another, feeling that all were equal under the common head—working women? Would we not most naturally co-operate for the good of all? Of course we know we are not good enough for all that, but we might try.

I think, too, with a member of the Steadfast Club, that working girls should meet in a social way, and that the clubs just meet this need, where they may come to-

gether for mutual improvement
and pleasure, being strengthened
and encouraged, and so start out to
work refreshed and brightened,
more hopeful and with more faith
in one another. Have we not
learned this through co-operation?

H. J.

After reading the papers, it
seems to me that we understand
pretty well what others owe us in
the way of kindness and good
will, and we also confess that these
duties are not one sided, but mutual. Now comes the practical
part ; to carry out these ideas in
daily living is far from easy. Self
interests and selfishness and laziness often stand in the way. We
need a Higher Power to give us
the will and the strength to overcome these tendencies.

We must expect annoyances in
this life. Don't place a stumbling
block in your fellow-workers' way,
and if a stumbling block is placed
in your pathway, don't fall over it.
but go around it.

The following points in one of the papers I think ought to be copied by each one of us and placed in our pocketbooks, where we can often see it : About being conscientious about our work ; that we should be ashamed of being inefficient and expecting people to repair our neglect. About faithfulness to the interests of our fellow-workers. I think this feeling ought to be as binding on us as patriotism is to the citizen. Many of us have not been taught to think. It is a great trouble to do so. It means effort on our part, and it is much easier to let someone else do the thinking for us. As has been said, we need clear thinking and prompt doing and all working together to accomplish what we desire.

The army ant is a little insect, but coming in an army with millions of others, it causes the flight of the largest animals. It is easy to praise our friends, but what they need from us is honest criticism and urging on to better things, surpassing present effort.

I. T.

Thoughts.

By being kind, considerate, and careful not to wound each other's feelings ; always speaking well of others, trying to help them in trouble, cheering them and making them contented with their lot.

We should try to set a good example, especially when we are provoked and feel like saying anything but kind, right things.

When we meet one another on the street, we should not look at one another distantly because not dressed, for some girls seem to be ashamed to recognize others in their working clothes.

We should respect each other's occupations, and always recognize every working woman with equal respect.

We should always speak well of

each other, and should put the best construction upon anything said or done.

We working women should stand up for one another, especially when we are spoken of in a slighting way.

By kindliness, and being careful of judging other persons' actions.

By a good example, by advice, encouragement, sympathy, by being above all a faithful friend.

Cheering the sick by visits, and being bright when with them. In sickness also, going in and taking a hand at doing anything that is needed.

By being thoughtful for those we know to be poorer than ourselves, being careful not to hurt their feelings in any way.

A few sunny spots.

The satisfaction of duty faithfully performed. Friends to advise and sympathize.

The advantage of cheap good reading.

When people working with you are pleasant.

A bright spot comes into a working girl's life when she finds that her best efforts are fully appreciated by her employer, and she feels that she is giving more satisfaction than a mere soulless and brainless automatom.

When a girl has her health, is willing and contented to do her work, receives a reasonable salary, and takes all the fun she can get.

When we win the good will and esteem of our fellow-workers and friends. When we feel blue, to meet unexpectedly some sympathetic friend. When we do unselfishly some kind action.

CHAPTER XIII.

DEFINITION OF CERTAIN WORDS.

Persistency.

THE idea of going on is given in the words, continue, persevere, and persist. Persistence is often used in a bad sense, and gives the idea that the one who persists will get what he wants, whether it is right or wrong. Perseverance is always used in a good sense.

Nothing can be accomplished without perseverance; it means keeping on and working till the work or object we planned for is attained.

When we hear or read about remarkable men and women, we

notice that they possess this quality in a marked degree.

Certainly, Columbus showed
perseverance during those long
years of waiting before he found
the king who would help him
discover a New World.

Take the case of one who died
not long since, Cyrus Field, and
his efforts and disappointments
in the laying of the Atlantic
Cable.

Palissy, the potter, determined
to discover a way of enameling
pottery. He brought his family
almost to the verge of starvation
in his efforts to do this, but
after sixteen years' work and
great hardships, succeeded, and
even now his wares are highly
prized.

But we need not go to the great
people of this earth to learn that
perseverance is important. Everyone who has a work to do must
persevere, or he or she will never
succeed.

The student must keep on;
even if his talents are moderate,

for if he has a great deal of perseverance, he will overtake his more brilliant companion.

Insects show perseverance in their work. The coral insect, working day and night and in countless numbers, build up the islands of the Pacific.

The ant and the spider work, no matter how often their labor is destroyed by man or the elements.

Now, how to attain perseverance:

If we have a work to do, we must consider the importance of the work; there must be some impulse to drive away laziness, which may be duty, ambition, or personal gain. Many times one needs a little encouragement, and the work goes on easier.

The hope of reward is one encouragement.

The will must be exercised in keeping on with disagreeable work. Ideal work is work done for the love of it, without hurry, fatigue, and without discouragement; but that sort of work is not found on this planet.　　H. J.

To be able to write upon this subject, one must possess to some extent that quality in order to do full justice to it, and as very few people can boast of that qualification, I am afraid you will have to be a little lenient. In order to persevere in all our undertakings, we must first of all possess a great amount of patience, and secondly, a certain amount of good-nature, for the one without the other would hardly justify our end, and before the object sought for could be acquired, our lack of good-nature would undo all our perseverance accomplished.

Perseverance depends greatly upon the amount of patience one possesses, for ofttimes one has a thing to accomplish which at first seemed impossible, but by continual perseverance, and not becoming impatient upon finding that one is not as successful as had been expected, and by trying

over and over again, your perseverance will eventually be re-
warded by success. To be per-
severing one must also be independent, for the moment one
depends upon others for the carrying out of an idea or an undertaking, they will never accomplish
anything, but will be just as far
off at the end as at the beginning.

No matter how hard a thing
seems, take it up cheerfully and
say, I will try to do the best I can;
and if we fail we can say, It was
not the lack of perseverance which
caused the same; and by constant
efforts of that kind, we become
accustomed to fight our own battles and to struggle against hardships which we are bound to come
across, and which good-humor
and perseverance will serve to
alleviate.   M. Y. B.

Independence.

One should try to rely on herself for everything, not to depend
upon others in everything; to
know how things should be done.

True independence is being able to pay your way through the world and not to depend on others.

To feel we can get along without others.

True independence in a woman is what it would be in a man if he were in her place without being a woman.

To be self-reliant and determined to support one's self, no matter how hard the work is, and willing to be helped as well as to help.

True independence rides in no carriage, makes the best use of his sturdy legs, but does not despise those who need crutches, and is glad to help an unfortunate traveler over a dangerous place.

True independence means entirely working and doing for yourself, keeping yourself respectable, and living an honest life. A person with ambition is always independent.

Having proper self-respect without overasserting one's self, or demanding more than one's just due, and not putting up with less.

Independence is self-support.

True independence is doing what is right, regardless of what others may think.

True independence consists of being self-reliant; but we must rely on God, as we can do nothing without his help.

Sticking up for your rights at the proper time, without making yourself disagreeable to those you come in contact with.

By doing your duty in the position you are put in, to the best of your ability.

True independence in a woman consists in living her life dependent upon the noblest and purest thoughts and feelings her conscience and heart may dictate.

I think that self-respect is true

independence, also self-government and self-control. If we
possess these, we will have cool,
clear heads, and can see best how
we can make the most of our own
lives and help others.

True independence is a proud,
"standing alone" feeling. To me
there seems to be no true independence, as everyone is more or
less dependent upon other people.

Co-operation.

Co-operation is where two or
more are banded together to help
their own and others' interests.

A mutual alliance, which helps
self and others, physically, men-
tally, and temporally.

Co-operation means working in
harmony. It is having an object
in view and all contriving to secure it.

Co-operation is strength in
helping one another; it is a
banding together, to better our

condition and to make us stronger.

Co-operation in its true sense is not only a working together of many for the many, but a disinterested, unselfish thing for each other's good individually.

It is a mutual working together of two or more persons for the furthering of the interests of the parties concerned.

To secure it, money is not alone needed, rather brains and sociability.

Co-operation is another definition of the Golden Rule.

CHAPTER XIV.

CLUB LIFE—ITS POWER.

IT seems a little thing to say that the Club has taught one to think, has roused one to thought. In our busy lives, we say we have so little time to think, but after we have belonged to a club a while, it is astonishing to find how much time we have to think, and how much we can think of in a very short time; also that it is the busiest people who think most, and are the people whom you can rely on when anything is to be done.

Thoughts are like pebbles thrown into the river: just how deep they go or just where they strike we do not know; all we can follow are the ever widening circles, and even they are lost to view in a little while. No one but the Supreme Being is able to tell how small or how great an influence they carry with them, or how far the influence will extend. When we are at work and happen to look up with a sudden smile and catch a neighbor's eye, and they ask, What means the smile they caught, we say, Well, you see, I was feeling rather low in my mind last night, and thought I would go to the Club, which I did. I can hardly explain just what it is that makes me feel better: sometimes I think it is in the atmosphere of the rooms; again, it seems the pleasant smile or jolly word or two; then again we have our " Practical Talks," which give me food for days sometimes, but above all, I think, is the oneness, if I may put it so. There's almost every kind of work represented at the Club, and some of our members don't have to go out to earn their daily bread ; we all meet on the common ground of woman-

hood and sisterhood; we mutu-
ally bridge over a chasm which
many people smiled on incred-
ulously some time ago, and
some even said it could not be
done without injury to one or the
other. Happily for us we proved
that it could be done, and it has
been working successfully now for
some years, and the injury has not
appeared; the Club working girl
does not feel that she is looked
down on, but feels she has gained
the respect, love, sympathy, and
loyalty of a stanch friend, while
the woman of leisure feels she has
gained a true friend in the girl
who has to go out in the world
alone day after day, who has
learned so well how to help herself, and is such a true, womanly
woman; for there is something
strong and self-reliant about her;
she is to be trusted.

If ever I feel blue, let me go to
the Club, if only for a half hour,
and I will feel differently when I
come out. It wakes me up, puts
new life in me, and gives me pleas-

ant thoughts for the morrow, and what seems a trouble before, melts into nothing, and you wonder at yourself for having thought that it did.

In our " Talks," we exchange thought and opinions, thereby gaining help and hints that prove invaluable.

Do you wonder, then, at my smiling to myself when I have such pleasant things to think of— why it makes me feel light, and my work seem easier? Then, too, I have so much to tell those at home that we don't have a chance to get rusty or fall behind the times ; meeting so many different girls, you learn something new almost every time you meet them, and that creates such an interest that your folks look for it almost as much as you do.

It is wonderful how your little store of knowledge increases—you learn so much more than you are conscious of at the time.

Yes, the dear old Club, I fear I couldn't do without it ; it does me

so much good and gives me such
strength and courage that to lose it
would seem as if half the light of
my life were gone ; the Club is so
necessary to me that I must make
myself necessary to the Club.
God bless and prosper our dear
old Club always.   I. T.

A club is a meeting place for
girls for mutual improvement.   It
is a place where by co-operation
busy women can secure advantages not otherwise possible.   It
can only start when there is a desire on the part of a number for
such a society.

It is a social gathering place to
meet one another, a membership
of love.   A place where we meet
to advance ourselves and help to
advance others.   It is a second
home, a place to know yourself
and others too.   A place where
we meet with kindness, receive
benefit, and go away feeling
strengthened.

The Club has always helped

in educating us practically, has taught us not only the qualities of ideal womanhood, but how best to strive to live an ideal woman's life in our small way. It has filled a long felt want in having a place to spend a pleasant and profitable evening at a small cost. Has also aided in creating true and lasting friendships. Has further taught us to look for all there is highest and best in one another.

It has improved the mind, encouraged the girls in many ways, and helped them out of many difficulties.

It has helped to educate us, and also helped me to overcome self-consciousness, and to try at least to look at the bright side of life.

It has made friends for me and taught me a great many useful things.

It has helped me to take a deeper interest in everyone, and has made us feel kind and friendly one with another.

It is a most pleasant feature in a working girl's life, and educates on many useful practical subjects coming into everyday life.

Club life enlarges our circle of friends, helps pass some cheerful hours, keeps us informed on what happens outside our workrooms, helps us to improve our mind by the classes, and does many other things too numerous to mention.

Club life has made us stronger, better women.

It has elevated the working class in the minds of the world in general.

As a closing word one member writes

EVERYTHING.

END.

GRACE HOADLEY DODGE

TEACHERS COLLEGE RECORD

| Vol. XVI | MARCH, 1915 | No. 2 |

GRACE HOADLEY DODGE

THE INFLUENCE OF MISS DODGE ON TEACHERS COLLEGE[1]

BY DEAN RUSSELL

To-day begins a new epoch in the life of Teachers College. During our holiday vacation Miss Dodge passed away and with her death closed an era in our history. From the beginning until now she has been a patron, friend and mother to us all. Not a day, certainly not a week, has passed since I became one of this group that she has not befriended in some material way a Teachers College student or officer. We owe to her our students' emergency fund that has restored to health hundreds of beneficiaries in hospital or sanitarium. She has been the backer and chief supporter of our religious and social work, and in a thousand ways, characteristic of her gentle nature, she has guided us to a higher life. Her spirit of consecrated devotion to the alleviation of human suffering and the elevation of human ideals is so incarnated in our institutional life that it must abide with us as her most sacred legacy.

Teachers College is the product of two confluent streams. One originated with President Barnard and flowed on to us through later presidents of the University: this is the idea of professional training for teachers as part of the work of a great university. The other stream started with Miss Dodge's interest in the girls and boys in the New York public schools. She saw them restricted to a narrow academic course of study and she longed to give them something that would add to their efficiency after

---

[1] An address given at a service in memory of Miss Dodge on Monday, January 4, 1915, in Milbank Chapel of Teachers College.

leaving school. With her to feel was to act, and to get others to act with her. She never hesitated to accept a good idea, no matter what the source, and she was ever ready to join forces with any one, however humble or however great, if thereby she might advance the cause to which her heart impelled her. When she was called to befriend the girls and boys of New York City, she found the Kitchen Garden best suited to her needs. She used it. This was soon merged into the Industrial Education Association which conducted an active propaganda for the new education wherever its publications went. Finally, she realized that the best help that can be given to boys and girls is to fit them to help themselves. This means school training under competent teachers, teachers more competent than those through whom she had tried to work. Her attention, therefore, was directed to the training of teachers. Then it was that Teachers College came into existence, an institution which President Barnard had foreseen with prophetic vision but which awaited the time when Grace H. Dodge should energize it with her dynamic power. That power consisted in her ability to put her whole self into any undertaking that appealed to her and, by her personal example of faith in the righteousness of her cause, to command for it the support of others. So with the venture of a Teachers College. She never doubted its success because she believed in its mission. And she believing as she did, others could not doubt. She gave lavishly of her means and she induced others to give. For many years, actually until within the last fifteen years, the annual deficiency in current expenses exceeded the total income from students' fees and endowment funds. When I came here, students paid eight thousand dollars a year and friends of the College were called upon for eighty thousand. But Miss Dodge, as treasurer, always prided herself on closing the year out of debt. New buildings were added to our plant and expenses mounted year by year to undreamed of totals, but she never wavered in her faith or lost confidence in the ability of our trustees to meet these obligations. When one great gift after another came, she accepted them calmly as in answer to her prayers—not for herself, but for us and our work. And herein is the secret of her life and of her success. She worked for others; for herself she wanted nothing—not even the grateful recognition of her service. In this spirit she gave us our Household Arts Building in memory of her mother, and in so doing indicated her abiding faith in the ideal of practical education which first led to her interest in Teachers College.

No words of mine can convey to you what the association with Miss Dodge during these past seventeen years has meant to me. She met me at the door when I first entered the building and in spirit, if not in actual presence, she has been at my elbow every day since. Sagacious in counsel, temperate in action, steadfast in affection, inspiring in courage, and sublime in her faith, hope and charity, she has been to me a tower of strength. But more than all else she has opened to me a view of that higher life in which the saints of earth and heaven dwell. Her example has demonstrated to me the futility of much that this world treasures and the imperishable value of some things that are commonly reckoned as of little worth. In her name I bid you share with me the spiritual bequest which she leaves to this institution.

Let me read to you a few words already familiar, but hereafter suffused with new meaning because of her life and work. You will surely realize, as I do now for the first time, why the recent translators of the New Testament sought to substitute the word "love" for "charity." It is clear to me that neither is sufficient. What is wanted is a word that will denote the greatest thing in the life of Grace H. Dodge.

"Though I speak with the tongues of men and of angels, and have not charity, I am become as sounding brass, or a tinkling cymbal.

"And though I have the gift of prophecy, and understand all mysteries, and all knowledge; and though I have all faith, so that I could remove mountains, and have not charity, I am nothing.

"And though I bestow all my goods to feed the poor, and though I give my body to be burned, and have not charity, it profiteth me nothing.

"Charity suffereth long, and is kind; charity envieth not; charity vaunteth not itself, is not puffed up.

"Doth not behave itself unseemly; seeketh not her own, is not easily provoked, thinketh no evil.

" Rejoiceth not in iniquity, but rejoiceth in the truth.

" Beareth all things, believeth all things, hopeth all things, endureth all things.

" Charity never faileth: but whether there be prophecies, they shall fail; whether there be tongues, they shall cease; whether there be knowledge, it shall vanish away.

" For we know in part, and we prophecy in part.

" But when that which is perfect is come, then that which is in part shall be done away.

" When I was a child, I spake as a child, I understood as a child, I thought as a child; but when I became a man, I put away childish things.

" For now we see through a glass, darkly; but then face to face; now I know in part; but then shall I know even as also I am known.

"And now abideth faith, hope, charity, these three; but the greatest of these is charity."

Yesterday I watched the sun set behind our western hills. As it rapidly descended I saw the shadows lengthen, fill the valley and stretch out eastward until they leaped the horizon. And I thought of the saying that an " institution is but the lengthened shadow of a personality." May the shadows cast by that noble life which has just reached its setting flood our valley and stretch away eastward till they leap off into the infinitude of time carried in the hearts of Teachers College students to the ends of the earth.

GRACE H. DODGE AND THE MAKING OF TEACHERS COLLEGE[1]

BY SETH LOW

I count it a privilege to be permitted to preside at this meeting in memory of Miss Dodge, because for the twelve years of my presidency of Columbia University, her co-operation and friendship were of much moment to me; and in the larger aspect of her life, I look upon her as one of the great women of her time; and she was as good as she was great. It was certainly a

---

[1] An address given at a service in memory of Miss Dodge on February 8, 1915, held in the Young Women's Christian Association Building, New York City.

prophetic insight of her parents that led them to name her Grace, for, as she grew in years, she developed every beautiful grace of character and of womanhood.

I know not how to describe that peculiar quality in her welcome of a friend, that happy blending of friendliness and welcome, better than to say just what it was, that it was graciousness, as if the fine soul in her saw only what was good in her friend and gave to that the right hand of her fellowship.

Miss Dodge has made her mark on the life of the city, on the life of the country, and on the life of the world. Others will tell you of her work for the girls' clubs; and I hope of her work for the Young Women's Christian Association, although that Association, in its modesty, has asked me to say little of it myself. They will tell you also of her work for students all over the world, and of her interest in missions. Let it be mine to tell you something of her work for the Teachers College, because for twelve years I was associated with her in that.

As one looks upon the Teachers College to-day, occupying with dignity and usefulness a large city block, one is tempted to take it for granted as a heritage from the past, like Columbia itself; but we owe the Teachers College to Miss Dodge more than to any other one person. I should be very false to her if I gave you the impression that she had done it all. Like every other great work, it represents the strivings and efforts of many devoted people; but, after all, in every enterprise there is one pivotal person, and no one who knows anything of the Teachers College will doubt for one moment that Miss Dodge was the pivotal person to whom we owe the Teachers College as it is to-day.

Now let me tell you how that came to be; because in doing so very simply I can make clear to you, I think, the remarkable combination of qualities which made Miss Dodge the influential person that she was.

In 1880 three or four young women, of whom she was one, perhaps twenty-three or twenty-four years of age, associated themselves in the Kitchen Garden Association. Their object was to teach household economy to poor girls so that they might understand better how to take care of a home when they came to have homes. Immediately two qualities showed themselves, which remained with Miss Dodge to the last, earnestness and enthusiasm. If she had not been earnest, if she had not seen the seriousness of life and wanted to be of use in it, she never would have entered upon such an undertaking; and if she had not had enthusiasm, she might have put her hand to the plow, but she would soon have let go.

Now those four young women received in their work some encouragement. There were plenty of pupils and there were some friends who helped to support it; but they very quickly learned two things, which I think betokened the presence in perhaps all of them, certainly in Miss Dodge, of three other qualities that are worthy of note. They learned first of all that kitchen gardening, or household economy, was only a very small fraction of a very large field; and they also learned that it was very, very difficult indeed to get teachers competent even to teach kitchen gardening in the way they thought it ought to be taught. So, then, we find them brought up to the problem that thus came up before them, a sort of problem coming out of the darkness of difficulties, like that beautiful thought of Blanco White in his great sonnet on " The First Day and Night." When he depicted the effect on Adam and Eve, of the coming on of darkness, you remember, he said of the first night, "And lo, creation widened to their view   .   .   ."

Now they found themselves in difficulty, in the clouds, as it were, and they did not know what to do. Then there came into play these other qualities, and first of all, great intelligence. They had the wit to perceive that, despite their difficulties, or perhaps, because of their difficulties, they were dealing with a little bit of a large problem instead of just attempting to carry on a philanthropic enterprise which might do a little good for a few years and then pass away. Having realized their problem with that sort of intelligence, Miss Dodge revealed, certainly, as perhaps the others did, a quality that is an essential part of all greatness. The scripture says, you know, " That he that would be great among .you, must be as a little child "; and I sometimes think that that means that to be great, you must be teachable. Now, it was a notable quality with Miss Dodge to the very end, that she never thought that she knew very much about these things. She was always ready to learn; and so, finding herself

in the presence of this enlarging problem, she was willing to
take good advice, and wise enough to know where to go for
the advice. Then, you know, or at some time very early in
her work, I am sure, there came to her a vision that the difficulties of this problem one day would be wisely dealt with;
that there would be teachers who were capable, because they
were trained, to teach household economy well; and to teach
other industrial arts well; so that in three years from the foundation of the Kitchen Garden Association it had enlarged itself
into the Industrial Education Association, and then a new thing
happened. They perceived then, with their broader outlook, even
more clearly than they had before, that it was hard to get
teachers properly trained to give industrial education, not simply
in a small field, but in the large field of all vocational training.
And so this Industrial Education Association set to work to found
a school that would teach such teachers; and the inevitable thing
happened again with people of that sort, they realized that what
was true of industrial training was equally true of all kinds of
teaching, that there was a lack of the most highly equipped teachers in every department in which good teaching was desired, and
out of that came the Teachers College.

It got its preliminary charter in 1889, nine years after the
seed thought was put into the ground in the shape of this
Kitchen Garden Association. In 1892 it received its permanent
charter. In 1893 it became affiliated with Columbia, and later
still more closely affiliated.

For one reason or another, I think all of the original workers with Miss Dodge had by this time fallen away, and when
Miss Dodge found herself with the college charter on her hands,
then she had need of still other qualities. She had them; as
her need was, so her day was. She needed, first of all, tremendous
courage. Think of the courage necessary to establish a college
for the new ideal, a college for a new purpose, and to build that
up right here in the city of New York; but her courage, like
the courage of a bird as it flies, was instinctive, and she flew
towards her mark with a flight as undeviating as a migrating
bird. Then she needed great perseverance, because you cannot
found a college over night; and year after year, year after year,
Miss Dodge was working for the Teachers College. She needed

other qualities and these other qualities came at her bidding. She developed the quality of leadership. I do not know of what that quality is composed, that capacity to lead, but I know what it does. We say that a leader must have magnetism, and certainly he must. Anyone who is to lead in a great enterprise must have the capacity to inspire others, and that gift Miss Dodge had with all her other gifts. She inspired first one and then another, until she associated with herself many men and women under her guidance; and then she needed and had that absolute self-forgetfulness that makes the followers of a great leader think not so much of the leader as of the cause. They follow the leader because the leader to them embodies the cause. That leadership Miss Dodge gave to the Teachers College. Then she was so situated that she could give generously to it, and she gave of her means as freely as she gave of her life.

When the Teachers College was first affiliated with Columbia University, there were 69 students in it, and about 300 who were not candidates for a degree. At the present time it is ministering to over 7,000 every year; where there were 69, there are now 2,000, and where there were 300 there are now 1,500, and others are reached in great multitudes through the summer school, and by extension teaching. There are in the college about 3 students sent by the government of India; there are 13 Chinese students learning how to teach and trying to grasp the ideals of the college; there are students from Japan; there are students from many of the countries of Europe; there are students from South Africa and there are students from every state in the Union, and all its outlying possessions.

That is the fruit of this little seed thought of Kitchen Gardening; Miss Dodge helped also to develop the flower, which was the Industrial Education Association; and this Teachers College is its rich fruit for the healing of the nations.

I want you to realize that year after year men and women competently trained, not only for the household arts, but for all other industrial arts; and for instruction in the humanities, in the classics, in the mathematics, and in the natural sciences, are going out of that college up yonder on Morningside Heights into every school district of the United States. There is not to-day a force in the Union as great in its effect upon the popular education of the United States as the Teachers College; and we owe that to our friend Miss Grace Dodge more than to any other one person, in memory of whom we are here. The Teachers College is only one of her monuments; but it is an enduring one, more enduring, as Horace said, than brass.

IMPRESSIONS OF MISS DODGE

BY LUCETTA DANIELL

No account of Miss Dodge's life would be complete which failed to give some consideration to the influences which led her into her lifelong work for girls and women or which did not include some mention of the more personal and intimate side of her life.

Miss Dodge often said that her first impulse for all kinds of religious and social work was received as a young girl in her parents' home where the great workers in all lines of social and religious uplift for the world.were constantly received as familiar and valued friends. Such men as Dwight L. Moody, the great evangelist, Henry Drummond, and President Gilman made the Dodges' home their headquarters whenever they visited New York and had an immense, though doubtless unconscious, influence on a nature already committed by a long inheritance from both parents to a life of service for others. Mr. Moody especially stirred her longing to give such service.

One of her most notable characteristics was her tendency to assume personal responsibility for any recognized need. And it was this characteristic that led her to form her first club for working girls. As a girl herself, buying of the girl across the counter, her sympathetic imagination put her into that other's place, and, as she said, " I felt ashamed that I had so much and she so little!" This first club was the forerunner of the whole body of Working Girls' Societies founded later in many states, and out of these in turn grew the vacation homes for girls. Equally characteristic of all the other movements she started was this tendency to grow,—to develop something new,—to have consequences. She always retained her personal relation to this first club, the Irene Club, named in memory of a young member who had died, and of whom Miss Dodge said, " One of the most beautiful characters I have ever known; I learned so much from her." Until a few years ago two evenings every month were devoted to this club unfailingly, whatever the weather or other demands might be. How many volunteer workers have such a record! To a friend who protested once against Miss Dodge's scanty annual fortnight of vacation, she said, "But my club girls would miss me so much if I were gone longer,—and my friends there can have only a fortnight's holiday,—why should I have more?" Her recipe for a successful club meeting is worth noting, —"Always too few chairs, then they have to sit on the floor and it's cosy!" She used to say, "I'm so happy with my club girls! I'm almost afraid of these learned college girls, they know so much. My club girls have not so much book knowledge and neither have I, but they have done so much living, and many of them have such fine characters that it is good to know and love them." And girls felt at home with her because of her simplicity, her sincerity, the genuine delicacy and respect with which she treated them. A friend happened to be with her one day when she received a letter from one of her club girls enclosing five dollars in payment of a loan. Miss Dodge sighed and said, "Oh dear! And you see I must let her return it, although she has walked back and forth to her work to save car fares and repay me,—because she is very proud and would be unhappy and hurt if I did not take it."

Another strong impulse towards work for girls, and so for the homes of the country, was gained from her experience as the first woman on the Board of Education, to which she was appointed when she was twenty-seven years old by Mayor Grace, who had always known her and believed her to be the one woman to take this difficult post. Her father, while willing for her to undertake this responsibility, insisted that some older woman must accompany her, and so Mrs. Richard Olney, an old friend of the family, was appointed with her. The shocking revelations of immorality existent in the schools at this time led her directly into work for the White Cross League, or social purity movement, and she has often said that Teachers College, with all its present world-wide influence, was the final outgrowth of a deep conviction that social purity must have its beginnings in the good home. The public schools were barren of anything

looking to this end, and so she associated others with herself
in a movement to provide instruction in various aspects of home
making, first through kitchen garden classes, and later, under the
Industrial Education Association, through work in cooking, sew·
ing, and housekeeping.

But probably the most potent influence of all in determining
Miss Dodge's lifelong consecration to the needs of young women
was the constant stream of individual girls sent to her from various sources for material or spiritual help, or friendly advice.
Every kind of need, sorrow or sin through which womankind can
suffer passed under her kindly ministrations, and with large-
minded wisdom she generalized from the individual case and
planned ways and means to prevent such waste for the girls of
the future. Her deep interest in the organization of the Travelers' Aid Association, to insure the safety of young women passing through the railroad stations of our great cities; in the Vice
Commission of two years back; in the American College for
Girls at Constantinople; and finally in the various departments
of the Young Women's Christian Association, religious and educational work, amusements, lunch rooms and housing,—all her
interest in such things as these is directly the result of her experience in dealing with individual girls and sympathetically
entering into the special needs of each.

A few incidents in the early history of Teachers College gave
Miss Dodge so much pleasure to relate that it seems almost impossible not to include them here. One is of the day when
the small chairs were being carried into the house on 11th
Street which was to be the temporary home of the kitchen garden. Miss Helen Burns, the superintendent and only worker,
was assisting the drayman when a sweet faced child with yellow
braids about her head stopped in passing and offered to help.
And she not only helped them, but eagerly joined the first class
formed. And this was Amy Schüssler! Another story Miss
Dodge enjoyed telling was concerning the opening of the Industrial Education Association at 9 University Place. Announce-
ments had been sent to all the public schools in the neighborhood
that on a certain afternoon classes in cooking, sewing, car-
pentry and drawing would be opened. But the whole thing
was experimental and all were nervously apprehensive that

it would be a failure. If no children appeared and the classes were not filled, the directors would have to close the doors of the association and reopen as a woman's hotel in the hope of recovering the heavy rental assumed. It was a crucial day. Miss Dodge spent the morning sitting about on barrels and boxes, overseeing the hanging of pictures and last preparations generally and then went home to luncheon. At the hour set for the opening she returned with an anxious heart. As she approached University Place she became conscious of a steady uproar of voices and found herself struggling through a mob of children that filled the sidewalks and the street from curb to curb and flowed around the corner into Eighth Street. The steps were impassable and she finally had to enlist the aid of a police officer to get her through the crowd of disappointed youngsters pounding on the door and clamoring for admittance to classes long since filled to overflowing!

Miss Dodge always took pleasure in speaking of the removal of Teachers College to the 120th Street site,—a step desirable in almost every way, but seeming to sign the death warrant of the young and highly prized alliance with Columbia University, then in its old quarters on 44th Street. Miss Dodge's own account follows:

"A Committee on Site and Building had been appointed from the Trustees, and this Committee had spent some weeks in studying localities, etc. They met one afternoon to report. The Chairman, Mr. Trask, said, 'We have decided that it would be well to think of certain lots in West 120th Street,' and gave many reasons why they seemed so desirable, but added, 'What is the use of thinking or talking of the matter when we have no money for land, much less for buildings, and certainly will not go into debt?' Mr. Vanderbilt asked a few questions, and in a quiet way, said, 'Telegraph now to the agent and say that if we can have the twenty lots for cash $100,000 we will take them, and I will pay the $100,000.' Within forty-eight hours the surprising announcement was made that Columbia University had bought the old Bloomingdale property and would move opposite the lots on West 120th Street. The widening of 120th Street was also announced, and the lots purchased for us by Mr. Vanderbilt

twenty-four hours earlier were worth $200,000, or double the
price paid for them."

Another story Miss Dodge loved to tell was of the anxious
time when the western lots fronting Broadway, where the Horace
Mann and Thompson buildings now stand, were offered for sale
by the owners and Miss Dodge as treasurer was straining every
nerve in vain to raise the amount necessary to keep them from
passing irrevocably out of our control. A day or two before they
were to be sold, a cablegram from New Zealand from Mr. James
H. Jones announced a totally unexpected gift of $20,000—enough
to save the day.

All who came into close association with Miss Dodge will pay
tribute to certain personal qualities which she possessed to a very
rare degree. One of the most striking of these was the combination of ability to handle the largest world questions in masterly
fashion, and yet to give unfailing attention to small details when
they were to contribute in any way to the welfare or gratification
of others. She was never too busy to send the note of apprecia-
tion for the smallest courtesy, or to plan ahead for flowers for
some sick person of whom she had only casually heard. And
the writer well remembers one beautiful drive when Miss Dodge
was quite uneasy at the end for fear she might be five minutes
late for the twilight reading before the fire on which a little boy
cousin was counting. She never broke a promise, she was never
late at appointments,—she had some marvelous system of records
which enabled her to recall on a given date a kindness done just
a year before and offer to repeat it. Her selflessness was so
genuine that she did not know she possessed it, and so entire
that she gladly and readily surrendered to the care of others any
piece of work into which she had put her whole heart, as soon
as she saw that it had arrived at a point where it would profit
most by their special contribution. She held positive views on
every subject, her own road was definitely marked out, but her
liberality for the views of others was truly astonishing, and her
money benefactions were only one phase of a generosity which
permeated her whole being.

But the tribute that would without question be dearest to her
heart if she could read what has been written of her would be
a recognition of the fact that it was the steadfast consecration

of her life to the ideal of the life of Christ that transformed
a nature which, though generous and lovable, was unusually
strong, masterful, impatient and very human, into a character of
such combined sweetness and strength as to prove without doubt,
even to those who shared her daily life—perhaps most of all to
them—the power of such an ideal faithfully followed. And
this is her greatest gift to us all.

Miss Dodge's Last Message to Teachers College Students[1]

When I was asked to come and talk to you to-day, my dear
friends, I wondered what I should talk about. I did not seem
to have any particular message. But I think that in these sad
times, when so many of our friends across the water are in
great anxiety and trouble, we need more than ever before the
Christmas spirit, which seems to me especially the spirit of quietness and peace. That is the Christmas message, you know,—
peace and quietness, and it is the message I should like to bring
to you to-day.

When Miss Miller asked me to come and talk to you again,
I asked her what I should say. And she said to talk about the
same thing I did last year,—health—and I think getting this
peace in our hearts is better for our health than anything else
we can do, better even than an operation! So many times we
forget this peace and quietness which may be ours for the
asking, and we are so anxious to accomplish all that we came
to Teachers College for and to get all the knowledge we can,
that we lose out of our daily lives some of these most valuable
things. I remember the first time this chapel was ever used.
Standing here talking to you, my dear friends, brings it all back
to me so clearly. That was the memorial service for Mrs. Wil-
liams, whose beautiful and wonderful life meant so much to the
College in those early days. And the dear friends who have
gone to Heaven make Heaven seem so near to us, and they
seem so near. We love them still and they love us. They know
what peace and quietness in the heart can mean to our daily
lives. It is so hard to get it and to keep it, you know. Some-

[1] An informal talk by Miss Dodge at a combined meeting of the Teachers
College Christian Associations held in Milbank Chapel, December 11, 1914,
as compiled from the recollections of several hearers.

times when I wake in the morning, I wonder if I can have peace enough to go around among the things that are waiting for me, and there are times when I have to strive to get the peace which will help me through the day. But I try to go out of my room possessed of the spirit of peace and quietness. Whatever happens will be God's will. He knows best. All we have to do is to trust the Heavenly Father. He has been so good to us. Faith in Him brings quietness and peace.

Then we must be careful about our health. We must be sure we have sleep enough. Some of us do not have enough. We think we can get along without it, but we must have it if we are going to do our work well and keep well. I wonder how many hours of sleep you need. They say some people need seven hours, but I need eight hours. And do we all realize that when we lie down at night there may be some people, perhaps some one in the very next room, who can not sleep because of something we have said or done? The influence that we radiate is felt by people somewhere all the time, even when we are asleep.

And if we do not have peace in our own hearts, we can not give peace to others. Don't you know how some people are always in a hurry, always so restless, and then how other people always give us such a feeling of rest and quiet and peace? I remember two women I used to go to see. One was Mrs. Josephine Shaw Lowell. Everything about her was so orderly and quiet and restful; she always had everything ready on her desk for you when you went in, your business was done in a few minutes, and you could come away feeling rested and helped. Then there was another friend to whom I used to go on business, and she was always in a hurry, and everything was in confusion, and you came away feeling as though you had been pricked all over,—it was all so unrestful, no peace anywhere. I have often thought of Bishop Lawrence, that busy man, coming all the way from Boston to sit in front of my fire and talk about Wellesley, the matter that was nearest his heart. He sat there talking as quietly as though he had all the time in the world. And in fifteen minutes he' had finished his business, and then he left.

It is very hard sometimes to keep peace in our hearts and

to have faith, especially at times when we are so anxious about our friends on the other side, some of our friends in the college at Constantinople, and perplexities here at home. But we know that all we have to do is to trust the Heavenly Father. We have always a friend there. He is so good. Many times in the history of our College we have had periods of doubt and anxiety, but just as in the past all has come out right, so we have faith that it will now. We must have faith in Him. And so this is my New Year's wish for you, my dear friends, that you may all carry peace with you.

I used to be able to have all the students at my home when the College was smaller. But now the College has grown so large, there are so many of you, that I have not room enough for even one club. I could not get you all into my home. I have to limit myself to having the foreign students as my personal guests. They can still come to me and I am so glad to see them. Here are two of my friends right here in front of me now. We have grown so large that we cannot all meet in any one place. Our friends are to be found all over the world. Dean Russell wanted to be here to-day, but he had to go to Maryland. And while we are meeting here, he is meeting with a group of our graduates in Baltimore. These friends of the College are carrying out the ideals we all believe in, wherever they are. I was never educated as you are. I never had an M. A., because I had to work. But I got my education by working with people. I can not have you all at my home, but I can come here and see you, and you can see me,—I am big enough for you all to see me! And though I can not call each of you by name, you are all my friends, and I love you all.

THE VARIED ACTIVITIES OF MISS DODGE

It is almost impossible to recount all Miss Dodge's activities, but it may safely be said that they all had their source in her interest in the lives of girls. With their welfare at heart, she busied herself with schools and colleges for them, a Christian association for them, and clubs, recreations and homes for them, seeking everywhere their development or their protection.

Teachers College was founded by her. She gave later the

Household Arts building and equipment, finished in 1910, a gift of approximately $500,000. She founded and supported the students' emergency fund and supported all religious and social efforts of the College. She was a trustee of the College from its founding until her death, treasurer for eighteen years, from 1893 until 1911, and served as chairman or member of important committees throughout its history. Her legacy to Teachers College amounted to $515,000 and one-sixth of the residuary estate. Her other school interest was connected with the American College for Girls at Constantinople, of which she was at the time of her death president of the board of trustees.

As a loyal supporter of the Young Women's Christian Association, she contributed to the new Lexington Avenue building, established the training school in New York City for Y. W. C. A. secretaries, and served as President of the National Board from its organization eight years ago until her death. She and her brother gave $625,000 in the recent Y. M. C. A.-Y. W. C. A. $4,000,000 campaign and she left a legacy to the Association of $700,000.

The working girls' clubs which are so numerous in New York to-day are the outcome of Miss Dodge's first club, the Irene Club; she was one of the founders of the Girls' Public School Athletic League in 1905, and founded the National Vigilance Committee about the same time; she organized the Travelers' Aid Association in 1907. She was a staunch supporter of the American Committee for the Abolition of State Regulation of Vice and of the American Purity Alliance. As the first woman member ever elected to the New York school board (1886-1889), she was largely instrumental in introducing industrial education into the public schools, and served in an important capacity on the Committee on Evening Schools. A library in Riverdale and its subsequent Neighborhood Association owe their origin to Miss Dodge.

Women in America

FROM COLONIAL TIMES TO THE 20TH CENTURY

An Arno Press Collection

Andrews, John B. and W. D. P. Bliss. **History of Women in Trade Unions** (*Report on Conditions of Woman and Child Wage-Earners in the United States,* Vol. X; 61st Congress, 2nd Session, Senate Document No. 645). 1911

Anthony, Susan B. **An Account of the Proceedings on the Trial of Susan B. Anthony, on the Charge of Illegal Voting at the Presidential Election in November, 1872,** and on the Trial of Beverly W. Jones, Edwin T. Marsh and William B. Hall, the Inspectors of Election by Whom her Vote was Received. 1874

The Autobiography of a Happy Woman. 1915

Ayer, Harriet Hubbard. **Harriet Hubbard Ayer's Book:** A Complete and Authentic Treatise on the Laws of Health and Beauty. 1902

Barrett, Kate Waller. **Some Practical Suggestions on the Conduct of a Rescue Home.** *Including* **Life of Dr. Kate Waller Barrett** (Reprinted from *Fifty Years' Work With Girls* by Otto Wilson). [1903]

Bates, Mrs. D. B. **Incidents on Land and Water;** Or, Four Years on the Pacific Coast. 1858

Blumenthal, Walter Hart. **Women Camp Followers of the American Revolution.** 1952

Boothe, Viva B., editor. **Women in the Modern World** (*The Annals of the American Academy of Political and Social Science,* Vol. CXLIII, May 1929). 1929

Bowne, Eliza Southgate. **A Girl's Life Eighty Years Ago:** Selections from the Letters of Eliza Southgate Bowne. 1888

Brooks, Geraldine. **Dames and Daughters of Colonial Days.** 1900

Carola Woerishoffer: Her Life and Work. 1912

Clement, J[esse], editor. **Noble Deeds of American Women;** With Biographical Sketches of Some of the More Prominent. 1851

Crow, Martha Foote. **The American Country Girl.** 1915

De Leon, T[homas] C. **Belles, Beaux and Brains of the 60's.**
1909

de Wolfe, Elsie (Lady Mendl). **After All.** 1935

Dix, Dorothy (Elizabeth Meriwether Gilmer). **How to Win and
Hold a Husband.** 1939

Donovan, Frances R. **The Saleslady.** 1929

Donovan, Frances R. **The Schoolma'am.** 1938

Donovan, Frances R. **The Woman Who Waits.** 1920

Eagle, Mary Kavanaugh Oldham, editor. **The Congress of
Women,** Held in the Woman's Building, World's Columbian
Exposition, Chicago, U.S.A., 1893. 1894

Ellet, Elizabeth F. **The Eminent and Heroic Women of America.**
1873

Ellis, Anne. **The Life of an Ordinary Woman.** 1929

[Farrar, Eliza W. R.] **The Young Lady's Friend.** By a Lady.
1836

Filene, Catherine, editor. **Careers for Women.** 1920

Finley, Ruth E. **The Lady of Godey's:** Sarah Josepha Hale. 1931
Fragments of Autobiography. 1974

Frost, John. **Pioneer Mothers of the West;** Or, Daring and
Heroic Deeds of American Women. 1869

[Gilman], Charlotte Perkins Stetson. **In This Our World.** 1899

Goldberg, Jacob A. and Rosamond W. Goldberg. **Girls on the
City Streets:** A Study of 1400 Cases of Rape. 1935

Grace H. Dodge: Her Life and Work. 1974

Greenbie, Marjorie Barstow. **My Dear Lady:** The Story of Anna
Ella Carroll, the "Great Unrecognized Member of Lincoln's
Cabinet." 1940

Hourwich, Andria Taylor and Gladys L. Palmer, editors. **I Am
a Woman Worker:** A Scrapbook of Autobiographies. 1936

Howe, M[ark] A. De Wolfe. **Memories of a Hostess:**
A Chronicle of Friendships Drawn Chiefly from the Diaries of
Mrs. James T. Fields. 1922

Irwin, Inez Haynes. **Angels and Amazons:** A Hundred Years of
American Women. 1934

Laughlin, Clara E. **The Work-a-Day Girl:** A Study of Some Present-Day Conditions. 1913

Lewis, Dio. **Our Girls.** 1871

Liberating the Home. 1974

Livermore, Mary A. **The Story of My Life;** Or, The Sunshine and Shadow of Seventy Years . . . To Which is Added Six of Her Most Popular Lectures. 1899

Lives to Remember. 1974

Lobsenz, Johanna. **The Older Woman in Industry.** 1929

MacLean, Annie Marion. **Wage-Earning Women.** 1910

Meginness, John F. **Biography of Frances Slocum, the Lost Sister of Wyoming:** A Complete Narrative of her Captivity of Wanderings Among the Indians. 1891

Nathan, Maud. **Once Upon a Time and Today.** 1933

[Packard, Elizabeth Parsons Ware]. **Great Disclosure of Spiritual Wickedness!!** In High Places. With an Appeal to the Government to Protect the Inalienable Rights of Married Women. 1865

Parsons, Alice Beal. **Woman's Dilemma.** 1926

Parton, James, et al. **Eminent Women of the Age:** Being Narratives of the Lives and Deeds of the Most Prominent Women of the Present Generation. 1869

Paton, Lucy Allen. **Elizabeth Cary Agassiz:** A Biography. 1919

Rayne, M[artha] L[ouise]. **What Can a Woman Do;** Or, Her Position in the Business and Literary World. 1893

Richmond, Mary E. and Fred S. Hall. **A Study of Nine Hundred and Eighty-Five Widows Known to Certain Charity Organization Societies in 1910.** 1913

Ross, Ishbel. **Ladies of the Press:** The Story of Women in Journalism by an Insider. 1936

Sex and Equality. 1974

Snyder, Charles McCool. **Dr. Mary Walker:** The Little Lady in Pants. 1962

Stow, Mrs. J. W. **Probate Confiscation:** Unjust Laws Which Govern Woman. 1878

Sumner, Helen L. **History of Women in Industry in the United**

States (*Report on Conditions of Woman and Child Wage-Earners in the United States,* Vol. IX; 61st Congress, 2nd Session, Senate Document No. 645). 1910

[Vorse, Mary H.] **Autobiography of an Elderly Woman.** 1911

Washburn, Charles. **Come into My Parlor:** A Biography of the Aristocratic Everleigh Sisters of Chicago. 1936

Women of Lowell. 1974

Woolson, Abba Gould. **Dress-Reform:** A Series of Lectures Delivered in Boston on Dress as it Affects the Health of Women. 1874

Working Girls of Cincinnati. 1974